To Margaret

I hope you ...
book,

Best Wishes

RJ Bell

AFRICA
ANIMALS
& ALISON

ROB BALL

with Natalie Ball

First published in Great Britain in 2009 by
Naturally Concerned Publishing
Naturally Concerned (for Alison) Ltd.
12 Stacey Grange Gardens
Rednal
Birmingham
B45 9PN
UK
www.naturallyconcerned.com

A CIP Catalogue of this book is available from
the British Library

ISBN 978-0-9564068-0-4

Cover designed and typeset by
Chandler Book Design
www.chandlerbookdesign.co.uk

Printed in Great Britain by the
MPG Books Group, Bodmin and King's Lynn

Female leopard looking disdainful

This book is dedicated to the memory of Alison.

I am tremendously grateful to Natalie for her help and support in this endeavour.

Her Mom and I have always been so proud of her.

Inquisitive Cheetah Cub

Acknowledgements

The writing of this book was both good fun and quite cathartic. I had great encouragement and assistance from many people. All of the errors are entirely my fault.

Thanks go to everyone who suffered me on the holidays and journeys. Alison was always the one to whom people were drawn. My sense of humour they received as a counter balance. For once, I don't think I have been too rude about anyone in this book. Nat even stopped me being too honest about the town of Oudtshoorn.

Liz Dollery, for whom the loss of Alison was also hugely significant, kindly read the draft and corrected me.

Working with Frankie and John Chandler has been instructive and critical to the book being published. Thanks guys.

The family encouraged me and kept me vaguely normal in the most difficult times.

Everyone was wonderful when Alison was ill and after she died. You will never know how much it meant to Nat and me.

Impala watchful

Lioness and package

INTRODUCTION

Lions doing the most natural thing in the Masai Mara

The male lion was gorging on the carcass of a recently expired wildebeest. As he lay, focusing on his task, a lioness walked over and growled in his ear. She turned and dropped to the ground expectantly. The male, which had a superb flowing mane screaming to the world his supreme masculinity, walked to her, copulated, bit her and got off. He resumed his meal. This process of procreation would be re-enacted twice an hour for four days.

Of course, I was in trouble with Alison for making a supportive off-the-cuff remark about classical male behaviour.

Wild animals are only driven to survive and procreate. They are naturally compelled to perpetuate the species.

Conserving the diversity of animal life is absolutely fundamental to the preservation of our planet. As a family, my wife Alison, our daughter Natalie and I have been fortunate enough to travel to Africa to see some of the most special creatures the world has, in their natural environment. These are experiences which cannot fail to inspire. Yet, there are still too many people intent on destruction of the habitat and slaughter of animals just for profit. For these people there can be no excuses; there must be action.

There is a complex situation in which local farmers are faced with starvation, loss of home and poverty if their cattle and goats are killed by predators. Understandable then, these people defend their property by slaughtering the big cats. Thankfully, there are enlightened schemes being developed to catch the animals and release them back into the wild well away from man. We are pleased to be able to support animal conservation projects. We have had the benefit of seeing the real thing.

The generic answer is Education. If uninformed individuals have no idea of the problem why should they change their behaviour? However, this has to be underpinned by clear laws which are fairly, rigorously and consistently applied.

So, why write this book? As this isn't a novel I don't have to keep the ending a secret, a final page surprise. Alison died in February 2008. This was the end of a chapter in the lives of Natalie and myself. We travelled extensively for twenty years from Fiji to Borneo, Lapland to Tierra del Fuego. However, we kept going back to Africa.

Alison was born in Nigeria, as her parents were living there, whilst her father lectured in Ibadan. The first five years of her life were spent there. She was never happier than when she was in the sun. Seasonal Affective Disorder (SAD) is speculated about, does it exist? Let me say it does and Alison had it. Her general humour was completely different when the sun shone from when she had the winter blues.

This book is focused on the "Dark Continent", Africa, or more explicitly our journeys to South Africa, Kenya and Zambia. Perhaps, even more accurately, watching animals.

I cannot square the emotional circle provoked by film of predators killing prey or another predator. The homily, "It's only nature" serves only to irritate me. I know, I've seen it many times before. That some animals have to die for the perpetuation of another is fact, but not a palatable one. I do not want to see a kill live. Seeing a carcass being ripped apart is different. If I thought that sausages were once a pig I would emote in the same way. Meat is not animal; it is ex-animal and, now, it is too late to rectify the situation. I offer this not as an excuse, just an explanation.

Wildebeest massing prior to a Mara river crossing. Alison clearly not expecting it to happen imminently

Particularly difficult to take, for example, is the death of a precious cheetah following a fight with lion or hyena. This is an action by the bigger creature to eradicate a competitor, which isn't logical as there are millions of wildebeest, small antelopes and zebra to eat. Rational doesn't apply, millions of years of evolution do.

Then there is the further moral conundrum of loving the wild and a compulsion to observe it, set against the impact of travelling there. Part of our answer is to be actively involved in animal conservation. This book will help fund that work.

Travel and animals were two of Alison's passions. I am very grateful we were never a family who saved for their retirement. We invested in the present, we made the most of our chances to go, see and do.

Female lion lies anticipating lunch

Book Structure

To explain the style of the book. Alison's and my final safari together was to the Mala Mala Reserve which abuts the Kruger National Park in South Africa. I am utterly confident this was Alison's favourite safari. We saw so much and enjoyed the whole experience enormously. Two months later she was in hospital having had the first seizures which were the initial clues that there were brain tumours. Therefore, I have used this last trip to act as the spine of the story. Each chapter reflects a separate drive in Mala Mala. The description of the drive is interspersed with reflections from other travels.

- The Mala Mala content is in this font Gillsans.

- Other South African reserves are described in Rotis Serif.

- *Kenya is in Gillsans italics.*

- The Zambian trip is written in Bembo font.

Using this approach has allowed me to combine linked issues and animals. Had I split the trips it would have become a repetitive list of specific animals and a mass of duplication.

At the end of each chapter there is a list of the animals observed on that particular drive, although as there are too many birds to record I have just noted those we hadn't seen in Mala Mala previously.

Finally, there is a short piece about a specific animal. This will, hopefully, allow the reader to understand a little more about some of the most amazing creatures on Earth.

Eagle-eyed raptor

Chapter One

GETTING STARTED

t is always the smell.

    With a little research someone could establish the components that merge to create this evocative odour. But why try?

    It's Africa.

    As the sliding door drew back there were two instant and simultaneous sensations. Firstly, something flew past my head at extreme speed, making me flinch and sparking my excitement register.

    It was a bat. It was 5.30am and these small vibrant mammals were highly active. Few people go on safari to see bats but to sense the first animal of the day before leaving the room was a great start. As there was only an initial glint of light on the horizon, it allowed the shape of the bats to be a mere impression. It was hardly a major sighting but it mattered to me. They were flying in big circles, presumably with a conscious intent. Or they just like flying and don't want to get lost.

    Secondly, there was that smell. Early morning and it was fresh, pure and inviting. We were on safari and we were about to go on a drive. If 5.30am sounds too early, I wasn't concerned at all; I would have been ready whatever the time. You don't go on this type of trip to stay in bed or lie by the pool (in the dark you may have to share the water with an unfriendly creature, anyway).

Adrenalin was surging - let's go now. Everything was enveloped by the prospect of viewing the game and that vague threat of danger.

"Do not walk alone at night, even in the camp."

Alison was taking a little longer to get ready. For some it appears it is always necessary to wear a touch of make-up and lipstick. My thoughts are more around not covering myself with smelly substances which could attract unattractive insects. Incidentally, do lions seek the more fragrant impala? Is deodorant, therefore, also an error by the female (and some male) members of the human race?

Impala waiting to be lunch

Natalie by our tents at Governor's Camp in Kenya

There was a rap on the door. Clearly, some people need awakening. One of the staff was there to escort us to snacks and coffee before the drive. As we walked the fifty yards it was impossible not to look for animals. They come into camp during the night but do these creatures know when it is time for us to get up and for them to retreat into the bush?

We were in the Mala Mala Reserve, at the Main Camp which has semi-detached, thatched rondavels for the guests. They are <u>really</u> comfortable. I actually prefer some of the tents in which we have stayed. In truth, "tent" is not the accurate picture. We have had four poster beds, en-suite loos, showers, hammocks and scented baths with glasses of sherry on the ledge. More importantly tents have noises, sounds of the night, if the air-conditioning is not too loud.

In the Masai Mara one year I was woken by a chomping sound right by my head. As Natalie was with us, and tents are for two people only, I was on my own. This strange noise had a very unnerving effect. I wanted to whisper to someone, to say, "I think it's a hippopotamus. Or is it something else?" Given hippos kill more people than any other animal in Africa, it is counter intuitive that I should actually hope it is one. However, I really didn't want it to be a large carnivore (or even a small meat eater). Rationally, it couldn't have been a problem as this animal was eating grass and shoots. Lions prefer meat, with a little extra side order of meat.

When the coffee arrived I asked the guy what it had been? It was a hippo; what a laugh, what joy. Only a hippo, inches from my head with a whole sheet of canvas between us. It is amazing how perspectives change.

The following evening as we arrived back at our accommodation, next to Alison and Natalie's abode, there was a big grey bottom protruding from the side of tent. They had to open the zip with the hippo three feet away and no hippo repelling canvas between them. For some hours the hippo remained around the tent, chewing the cud, bumping into support poles and breaking wind. I heard none of this as sleep came the moment I got into bed. Giggling went on for a long while, reportedly. The hippo wasn't affected at all. See what I mean about the attraction of tents?

The first time we stayed in a tent was at Savanna Lodge, also in South Africa. As ever I was sleeping alone. Personal habits not withstanding, it is still a little disappointing to be dispatched to solitude each time. My tent was the furthest from the dining area and civilisation. The charming woman escorting me around introduced herself as Celia. She reminded me of a giraffe; very tall, slim and exceedingly graceful. Do people mirror their surroundings, do they get a job there because of their looks or is it all a complete coincidence? As we walked, we talked;

Celia; "Please feel free to walk around camp during the day but you must be accompanied at night. It is just an extra safety measure."

Me; "Believe me I have no desire to be brave. Do you have snakes here?"

Her (laughing because I am an idiot); "Of course, but they want to avoid you as much as you want to avoid them."

Now this is very reassuring. Except, the first time we went on safari I read a travel guide on the plane which, when referring to camping, stated, "Be careful where you choose to pitch the tent as there are snakes EVERYWHERE." My emphasis is given here but the page pulsated at me. I hate snakes. And there was rustling in the grass next to Celia and me. A snake, she thought. I didn't go in to find out.

Hippos and crocodile seen from the dining area at Governor's

Cunningly, I had bought a robust walking stick earlier in the holiday. This was tremendously comforting on a personal level, the stick went everywhere that I did. People may have taken the mickey but I didn't care. With my cricketing skills any slithery reptile could have been dispatched rapidly to the boundary of the camp.

It is said that humour doesn't travel and, indeed, that may well be correct. It was only a small merry aside when I said to the junior ranger that this was, in fact, a Rhino Repelling Stick. He looked concerned and said he thought it was unlikely to stop three tons of rampaging animal bent on piercing my gut with its rigid horn. Is this true? Do South Africans have no sense of irony or whimsy?

Anyway back to animals in the camp. After the first drive of this particular holiday we arrived back after dark. Members of staff were there "armed" with large torches.

The guide was flashing his light all around, up and down.

Me;   "Are you looking for snakes?"

Guide; "Yes. But other things as well"

Inevitable question...

Me;   "Like what?"

Guide; "We get lions and hyenas in
        the camp."

Me;   "Are they the most dangerous?"

Guide; "No. They make a noise and give you
        a chance."

Me;   "So what is the worst?"

Guide; "Buffalo. They just hit you.
        Dead. No warning."

Family Breakfast

This was not reassuring. Subsequently, it has become clear that old, solitary, male buffalos are the problem. It is possible to sympathise with an outcast living alone, surrounded by others who wish to kill and eat you. Who wouldn't be cantankerous and prone to act first, then consider the broader implications at a later point?

As well as a walking stick we had also been joined by our friends Nigel and Mary Minett on this trip. This was sound thinking. No human being can out run a lion. The trick is to out run someone else. Lions do not have a logic which innately compels them to eat the fastest of a breed. Lions want food and the easier the better. The more people, the better the odds are you can beat someone to safety. The night stroll seemed to defy these precautions. I was, and still am, nervous in the bush after dark. This is their time.

A little nervousness is healthy, complacency is bad.

Respect the environment you are in. There is a well known plea but highly pertinent,

"Take only pictures, leave only footprints."

It is on postcards, posters, T Shirts and anything else possessing the space. Twee due to overuse but a sound adage for tourists.

Returning to Mala Mala, each lodge has great space, brilliant views and two bathrooms (his and hers for different odours and occupation time). Our window overlooked the pool area and across 100 yards of vegetation to the River Sand. To our left was the breakfast/lunch deck and past that an open area of grass. To the right was a wooded area, followed by the bending river.

Walking in the open areas was fine but, again, braving the bushes and shrubbery would have been plain daft. Bad things happen when you can't see dangerous animals, then they see you or you tread on one. Another of those well known "facts" is you do not see the snake that bites you. It has reacted to a foot landing on its back. You can be sympathetic. Snakes, such as the puff adder, have efficient camouflage for different reasons but being trodden on will be interpreted as an attack.

In our ten safaris we have only seen two snakes. Both times it was a Puff Adder. On the first occasion at Savanna the ranger, Paddy, jumped off the car and stepped into the long grass. He emerged poking the snake with a short stick. He herded it towards us for a good look - a close up. I am sure he was in control but bits of my body felt like they weren't. Six feet from the vehicle he relented and allowed a very annoyed Puff Adder to slither back to anonymity. The ranger and guide were amused; I wasn't. It was, of course, a point of honour to be apparently blasé, not to display horror at being too close to my bête noire.

The second time, the snake was slipping across the road and its progress was not interrupted by us. Good to see it, great to see it disappear.

South African puff adder in annoyed state

It may seem a little incongruous that I want to go anywhere there are snakes. In truth, excepting Ireland, that wouldn't leave many places to go. I cling to the maxim they are more scared of me than I am of them (so, they must really, really worry about me) and I still carry a stick and wear thick boots.

In the room in Mala Mala there were comfy chairs, a writing table, lamps, cushions and a giant bed. Alison and I could have avoided each other for months in the bed it was so big. Perfect for married couples. Of course, there was air conditioning/central heating. It can get very cold in winter. In reality, winter can also be a great time to go on safari. The vegetation is sparse and it is easier to see the game. Typically, it is dry and predators are active.

Just take more layers of clothing and accept it is chilly first thing in the morning. It isn't too cold, it is not like winter in Britain. Are you a man or a mouse? And before you answer remember how many creatures would see a mouse as breakfast.

Our real breakfast wouldn't be until after the game drive but there were coffee, tea, chocolate and biscuits as options before we went out "hunting". We always try to be available for the ranger to get going early, to beat the rush. However, if there are fellow guests in the same vehicle we are governed by the speed of the slowest. Rangers and trackers don't operate on Africa Time, they appear to be as keen as us to be out there.

It is always fascinating to ask the staff, "what has been in the camp in the night?" The answer on one occasion was a pride of lions chasing a zebra. On another occasion it was two male lions roaring. Alison and I slept through both occasions. Rarely is the answer nothing.

On a different occasion, Alison was in a camp with her friend Liz Dollery. At dinner there was a kerfuffle behind the kitchens. The staff took the guests to see some hyenas sorting through the dustbins. Truly, they are scavengers. This is also a good example of reasons I, and many others, dislike hyenas. They are on the same list as crocodiles and vultures. It is clear they are in the food chain, and therefore relevant, but they have disgusting personal traits which make me loathe them and be enthralled at the same time.

Talk at breakfast was stilted. Eager to move on, not knowing anyone and operating on six hours sleep we really had little to say. It would change by the end of the day and change wonderfully.

Whilst this was to be our first full day, in reality it had all started the day before, as we arrived. For the British, South Africa is great, in terms of time zones. It was only a two hour time difference, so no Jet Lag. It is quite a long flight, typically ten hours. Alison and I had caught a night flight and we were both able to sleep on planes quite well. She basically curled into a ball and became comatose until the descent into Johannesburg. I can't exactly replicate this with my much longer legs but I did get five or six hours of decent kip. We were relatively fresh even though it was early morning, on a new continent, in a different season. In South Africa it was early autumn and we had left an unseasonably hot spring in England. There were few difficulties progressing through immigration, given the forms had been completed accurately, by me as ever.

Our bags had also arrived safely. I emphasise here bags, not cases. Travel as light as you can. Dressing up is not the norm on safari and there are limits to the weight carried on the onward journey in a much smaller plane. Obviously, there needs to be some thought to the season. Is it going to be cooler, wetter or so hot it can burn in a few minutes? Again, the point should be made that this is not a holiday for sun seekers. The Canary Islands are available at a fifth of the cost if sun is the primary function for Rest and Recreation.

Luggage itself should be light in weight and experienced animal watchers will be carrying cameras, binoculars, and books to identify indigenous fauna. It can easily become a fact that there is little space for clothes. So wear layers for the journey, buy lightweight kit and realise it doesn't matter because there is no expectation of sartorial elegance. Do take enough to change into in the wet seasons. Usually, their summer has greater rainfall. Being on a drive when it rains is fun, even if there is a smidgen of discomfort. At home I always believed visiting zoos was better in the rain as animals were more active. This may be true in that context but now I avoid zoos and in the wild, if it is raining, the animals miraculously disappear.

At the airport it is necessary to transfer to the Domestic Terminal. This is a five minute walk, pushing a trolley. Depending on the travel company through which we have booked we have even been met, escorted and guided through check-in. Whilst this was welcome it isn't absolutely necessary as it is very straightforward.

The Domestic Terminal is new, fresh and pleasant. There are several places to snack, breakfast and drink coffee. Plus inevitably there are well stocked curio shops. An hour here is part of the whole holiday experience, stimulating more anticipation. Reading local newspapers (all of which have English Premiership football scores), hearing the accents and imagining the experiences to come. I had been trying to picture this particular future for months, now it was tantalisingly close. The process of travelling can be good fun; time to observe, consider and absorb.

At the time the Exchange Rate was quite good, so buying a meal was relatively cheap. Usually in South Africa the service is good. A small disappointment was the disinterest the waitress showed on this occasion. But who cares? Relax and go with the tide. My natural impatience can be subsumed by anticipation in these circumstances.

A short bus ride to the plane and on board. No delay, taxi to the runway and immediately soar into the air. Brilliant.

The plane probably seated 50/60 people. There was just one stewardess, who distributed a soft drink (it was mid-morning) and a cheese roll. This was luxury compared with previous flights in Kenya.

From Nairobi the transfer to Masai Mara is by a 12 seater plane with one pilot. It is incredible. Of course, any movement up, down or sideways can be felt more acutely but the sense of the moment is

heightened. It only takes an hour to the area but there are numerous landing strips in the Masai Mara, so we landed and took off twice before it was our turn to disembark. As we dropped to fifty feet a flock of vultures was shredding a carcass by the side of the runway. Welcome to gentile and subtle Kenya.

However, the real flying treat was to come on the way back to Nairobi. Remembering the plane was a 12 seater, we had 13 passengers; I was left on the tarmac whilst the others took their places. Gulp. Was I to be left alone on the ground? Would random man-eating animals arrive? Tune in next week...

Light aircraft which flew from Nairobi to Masai Mara

No, I was to be co-pilot. Or at least sit next to the pilot. This was superb. The views were spectacular. After two landings at other landing strips I was convinced we were all safe if the proper pilot had a heart attack - I could take over from him heroically. Perhaps not in fact but I did get a sense of the processes the pilot employed and I loved the whole experience.

Inevitably, I did announcements to the passengers. None of them were factual, none of them believed. How we chuckled *(or maybe not). Yet another example of my family cringing.*

I suspect more people are nauseous in smaller aircraft and fewer people enjoy these flights. However, for those of us who do find it a positive experience it is intensely stimulating. Soaring, but as the noise is quite penetrating, in a grumbling manner.

I did hand around the sweets to the dozen fellow travellers. Unlike some professional stewardesses I did not flirt with the (male) pilot. He was oblivious to the passengers as he was wearing his "cans" and talked frequently to ground control, or maybe his mate. There was no opportunity to discuss the finer points of aeronautical travel, to develop my growing confidence as a substitute flyer should needs be.

Mala Mala has the best runway we have seen in the Bush. Proper tarmac, long and smooth. It is the only way such a sophisticated plane could land safely. It did seem a bit disappointing, as it isn't the rugged experience we crave. There is nothing to stop a wild animal cavorting across the runway at any time. Many of the airstrips are basically dirt tracks. Perhaps you should not have read that bit if you ever think of going on safari.

The aircraft taxied the short distance to the parking area. There is no facility other than steps to disembark. The heat hit immediately. Wonderful and exciting. We were on holiday and what a holiday.

As a five year old I used to absorb books about Africa and the animals. It was always the big game I adored. Trips were planned to capture exotic creatures, so I could have my own zoo.

I grew up with pets. At one time we had a dog, cat, mice, rabbits, budgerigars, tortoise and goldfish. Less dangerous than lions but more practical in a three bedroomed semi-detached suburban house in Kings Norton, Birmingham. My parents were very accommodating. Every time I wanted a new animal I committed to looking after it diligently. Then I let them do all of the smelly work whilst I read a book or played football on the field at the bottom of the road.

Alison and I have had as many as nine cats at one time. This is a direct result of Alison working for Cat Protection as a volunteer. We became an annex. When she came home pleading for number nine the deal was that if he came home Alison stopped working as a cat helper.

My hunting plans constructed nearly fifty years before may have been grandiose and infantile but this was indicative of the underlying thrill I feel every time we go on safari. This is literally living the dream, childhood fantasies realised. It is like being in a television programme in three dimensions; visual, plus the sounds and smells. You can almost taste it as well. So far there hasn't been much touching of wild animals. That would be unfair for both them and us. Tales to prove the exception to follow.

All this just from getting off the aircraft. Does this trip have the potential for excitement or what?

One of our old cats was called What. Alison said, "Shall we call this one Bill or what?" Well, I didn't want Bill, so it had to be What. And what fun we had with What. Take him to the vet and naturally the receptionist asks, "What is the cat's name?"

"Correct. How did you know?"

"No, the cat's name is what?"

"That's it"

And I could keep it going for ages if Alison wasn't with me to temper my excesses. Strangely the receptionists never found it as amusing as I did.

But back to Africa - we waited at the "airport" impatiently. The cars arrived. Our bags went in one and we climbed into another.

Often the drive to the camp is in itself a mini-safari. On one occasion we saw three of the Big Five even before we reached our destination.

Leopard in Londolozi, South Africa

African buffalo taking water in Tanda Tula, South Africa

The Big Five are;
- Lion
- Leopard
- Elephant
- Buffalo
- Rhinoceros

These were the animals the Big Game Hunters sought most. May the ultimate demise of the hunters have been a painful one. Even recognising cameras didn't exist, killing beautiful living beings to satisfy the ego seems vilely excessive. And it is more than rumoured it continues today, for the very rich. Scum.

Everywhere there are references to the Big Five, it is an unspoken agreement to use the phrase to market Sub-Sahara Africa. Even in the bush there is Public Relations.

In Mala Mala the drive to the camp is very short and we saw nothing but bushes and trees. Still we were greeted by lovely people, offering chilled fruit juices. Many faces appeared, introductions made and, in my case, names immediately forgotten. I am hopeless. This reflects on me, not on them. I think it is because instead of listening I am thinking about my own first words. Can I be amusing? Well no, in all probability, but we live in hope.

Registration is uncomplicated and unsophisticated, except signing the Indemnity Clause - not their problem if you get eaten - and it is very quick. To the room and to unpack. No couple (or trio if Natty is with us) could make a room more untidy in a shorter space of time than us. Cupboards are for wimps, drawers are for the obsessive. Floors are for the true traveller to spread their attire. We are slobs, which is ironic given Alison's desire for order at home.

I opened the door to the patio for the first time and stepped out to paradise. I sat at the table I was to use to write my notes and savoured the view. A thousand plants I couldn't identify hid a million creatures I couldn't see. The Sand River flowed by a hundred yards away and we knew there were hippos and crocodiles in there somewhere. Birds soared at a height that meant they were unidentifiable to the rank amateur. I was here to listen, learn and observe.

Seeing an animal is not enough. Seeing an animal and taking a photograph is not enough. How do they behave, what do they do, how do they hunt, what do they eat, when do they become active, what sounds do they make? And many other questions, many of which only come to mind when the animal is seen or after it has gone.

On the other hand there are people, and the Japanese seem to be in this group, who prefer the manic rushed version of life. Take a picture, tick the box and move on to the next spot. They spend a fortune getting to South Africa, so it is their choice, just not mine.

It became a disappointment in Kenya, in the Masai Mara, that at every view of any animal it was surrounded by a dozen or more vehicles. It is now a zoo. A very big zoo indeed but a zoo none the less. The creatures are supposed to be living as they have done for many thousands of years. This would indicate Toyota and Land Rover were producing cars a long time before man invented the wheel. Animal behaviour has been adapted to our presence. Before the recent troubles it is estimated 138,000 visitors per year went to the Masai Mara. This is a vast number for the wild to accommodate.

Near our camp a leopard and cub had been seen in a small wood. It was late in the drive, nearing dusk. We could see a shape and some movement. It was a leopard and, therefore, we could claim a sighting. So could scores of other people surrounding the area. The animal could not escape if it wanted, and so it prowled and protected its baby.

Leopard mother and cub

Thankfully, all of the other vehicles left. It was, after all, time for a meal. Some people need to feed the inner man/woman rather than feed their soul. We stayed for a while longer. The reward was to see the leopards emerge from the undergrowth. It was time for a stretch and a wee. Alison was very excited; leopards were her favourites. These were really close. Their markings were precise and beautiful. This was a rare experience. It feels as if it is possible to get out of the vehicle and approach the cats. Not withstanding the stupidity of this action the threat is to the animals. The ranger would have to shoot them rather than lose a client. There is a story, which is probably apocryphal, of a Japanese man who walked over to a pride of lions. His wife continued to film as the man was eaten. Something to show the grandchildren. It isn't revealed how many boxes were ticked that day. The wife did win the prize at the end of the safari for dedication to her art.

The last bit is not true - probably.

So, we arrived in time for lunch after the flight in from Johannesburg. We were agog but the first drive wasn't until three o'clock. Therefore, we ate. The cuisine is a very high standard, a buffet with a great deal of choice. Alcohol is available but, and my friends will be amazed, I never have any desire for drink in the middle of a safari day. There is too much to see and do. I want to be totally clear headed, alert and be able to remember everything. This rule doesn't apply for the evening meal. South Africa produces some great wines.

The first drive; how do you stop time? Life rushes by us, a swirl of anticipation and memories. One is unclear because it still has to occur, the others gradually disappear however hard we try to keep them. Being in Mala Mala, our senses were heightened by possibilities, doing something we love.

The weather was glorious, hot and sunny. We dressed to cover, as sunstroke and sunburn do not enhance the experience. In the rucksack were extra layers for later, after daylight has gone and the temperature drops.

Our ranger was Andy, the tracker Marka, trainee ranger Sean and our fellow guest Mark Shapiro from Memphis, Tennessee. The large 4x4 could have easily accommodated another four people. The design is clever, having three different levels to ensure the best views for everyone. Being a large child I do like the backseat which is the highest but it does mean I don't hear everything the ranger is saying. Without exception the rangers have been brilliant and have endless patience. The same questions are asked time and again, sometimes on the same drive. Rangers all tell tales of similar levels of ignorance from the punters; "Can we see a tiger?" is the classic. Of course, shall we pack a hamper for the 6000 mile journey to a completely different continent?

So, we were off, camera, binoculars and pen in hand, relearning how to absorb the bumps from travelling over tracks rather than roads. Sway and hold on are the answers. It is part of the experience. As is the dust.

Large car for the drives with small Alison

On our first safari we travelled in a people carrier, a nine seater mini-bus. We had been picked up from our hotel in Mombasa in Kenya for a 5 hour journey to the Game Parks of Tsavo (East and West). If I am honest we loved it. Only after realising how good safari can be did we understand this first time was second or third division by comparison.

The Tsavo reserves are National Parks. This means cars have to remain on the roads and wait for the animals to come within spotting distance. In private parks the preference is for roads but occasional shortcuts are taken. The real difference relates to the knowledge of the guides. I spotted far more than our driver in Tsavo. He couldn't answer questions but thankfully he could mend a broken down vehicle - a skill needed before we reached Tsavo. At a petrol station as we stopped for mechanical improvements we were surrounded by youngsters asking for pens. Each of us had been made aware of this minor phenomenon, all children want pens, so we had come prepared. Less savoury were the tactics at local curio shops. Inevitably, Mr Hassan stopped at several (for his commission). One trick was to persuade the customer to believe a part exchange of old trainers meant a real bargain was being acquired. Whilst my trainers remained on my feet we did buy a painting of a herd of elephants which remains on our hall wall for people to see as they enter our house. A tip is think about the flight home and do not buy the frame.

The people carrier was a normal car but with a pop up viewing hatch to allow us to stand and see further. It felt more secure but we have never felt worried in a vehicle without a roof. In the Masai Mara the 4x4's do have a roof which opens to let people stand and cheetahs to hop aboard to see further to hunt prey (more about this later). So, why don't predators jump into the car and eat us? Apparently, they don't see people only the shape of the car. Rangers do insist people don't stand in open sided vehicles as Big Cats may realise their error. These animals have become completely relaxed in the presence of cars. They carry on as if we aren't there. This does re-enforce our responsibilities to keep the rules and protect the animals and their habitat.

Not unusually, we almost ran into a special creature. This time it was a young female lion. Andy knew she was a member of the Styx Pride. Although she was alone there was no concern that she was lost. Intelligence said she would call to the rest of the group if she felt any doubt. As it happened she was only yards from her family. The lioness had been sitting by the track when we arrived. Now she stood, stretched and moved slowly and languidly towards the other lions. Generally, lions do not rush. However, when they need speed it is instant, extreme and awesome.

Playful cub and fed up mother lion

We came across three lionesses with six cubs lying in the grass. Life was passing by in an apparently acceptable manner. Yawning was the most strenuous activity to be seen. As we approached, the lions espied a single hyena. Hyenas will kill lion cubs if they can. The logic of this is, as explained, being that it reduces the number of competitors for food. Lions are at the top of the pecking order, so have first pick.

None of the lionesses made an audible sound but absolutely clearly they communicated. One stayed with the cubs, whilst the other two set off in an arc towards the hyena. The hyena ran. The lions fanned out and went from 0 to 40 miles per hour in three steps. Unbelievable power and aggression. The chase finished quickly as the job was done. The hyena knew better than to come back. It did show us how rapidly things can change. Previously, I had been doubtful about claims a lion could be fifty yards away and, despite you being next to the car, it wouldn't be enough to save you. It may remain an exaggeration but not by much. We were blessed to observe a small example of raw intent and malice, translated into sinewy acceleration. Lions are fat free killing machines.

We followed the Styx pride at an indiscreet distance. There was a sense of purpose as the females moved towards a waterhole, in which a large male water buffalo was taking a mud bath. There were seven lionesses and one male lion. He lay a hundred yards away waiting for his just desserts. In doing so, he also avoided the danger of being hurt or killed in the inevitable fight about to happen.

Gradually, the girls edged towards the happily oblivious ruminant, to the point at which it seemed certain there would be

Watching lions surrounded by people

a scrap, a contest to the death. The oldest cat, the matriarch, went in first. And came out first as the buffalo reacted aggressively. The buffalo turned and strolled away. The lions didn't chase. There was another buffalo.

Buffalo bathes whilst lions watch

The second buffalo could not have appeared less concerned. It wallowed disdainfully. He emerged and pursued the potential predators up the hill to the area in which we had stopped. We sat amidst the action, feet from seven hungry carnivores, cameras ready to repel boarders and save ourselves from a random attack.

Buffalo Two took to the water where he played, taunted the lions, rolled on his back and deliberately bared his vulnerable stomach. Even the lions must have been upset at this display of indifference which verged on contempt.

The views of the master scornfully watching his harem were clear. He was hungry and irritable. His role in life is to watch, protect and impregnate but not hunt. That is women's work.

A huge herd of buffalo were moving by just beyond the scene of the lions' debacle. The rest of the herd didn't care either. The lions rose and followed the herd. There was a lot of noise but no killing.

It did promote the question, "Why were the lions so keen and so stupid as to want to kill a buffalo when there were scores of impala in the vicinity"? Impala are small antelopes, also known as breakfast or McDonalds, as it appears as if a letter M is painted on their bottoms. The answer probably has something to do with the fact that one buffalo is worth more than ten impala. Yet a buffalo is far more meat than this pride would eat.

Earlier in this first outing we had seen a young leopard, as yet not given a name by the rangers. She was lying in front of a bush, in which she had concealed a kill. We could see the remains of a male impala. Again, this is far more food than this one leopard would eat. Her immediate aim was to protect it from other predators and those creatures which live off the efforts of others, the carrion eaters.

It was an impressive kill as the antelope would have been twice the weight of the cat. The initial feed had been taken. We enjoyed the stench of the rawest meat imaginable.

The leopard was between two and three years old. Andy knew she was still living within the territory of her mother. It was likely this young creature would create her own domain, at least some of which would be taken from her mother. There would be no love lost between them after the period of separation that had occurred. It's a jungle out there.

Returning to the lodge we had to cross a ford at the River Sand. In the space of fifteen yards there were some beautiful birds; a hamerkop, a grey heron, a cormorant and a pied kingfisher. Not the street cred of big cats but glorious none the less.

Animals seen on this particular drive;

Pied kingfisher at Hamerkop Corner

MAMMALS

▦ Impala

▦ Leopard *1 female*
            1 male (known as the Bicycle Crossing Male)

▦ Dwarf Mongoose

▦ Elephant

▦ Lion *The Styx Pride*

REPTILES

▦ Rainbow Skink

▦ Leopard Tortoise

BIRDS

- Burchell's Starling
- Red Billed Hornbill
- Yellow Billed Hornbill
- Longtailed Shrike
- Swainson's Francolin
- Lilac Breasted Roller *(Alison's favourite - exquisite)*
- Cape Turtle Dove
- Hamerkop
- Grey Heron
- Cormorant
- Pied Kingfisher

ANIMAL OF THE CHAPTER;

- Leopard *(Panthera pardus)*

Leopard in Londolozi

34

Chosen for the first chapter because Alison loved them enormously. Leopards are very difficult to find because of their rosette camouflage markings, being typically nocturnal and by nature solitary.

Leopard eats in safety

Whilst the leopard is the second largest of the African big cats it does have a number of threats; lion, hyena packs, wild dogs which are always in a group, crocodiles and, of course, man, as we abuse the habitat and pre-emptively eliminate a dangerous animal. It has now reached a point where leopard is "near threatened".

DNA has established the link for leopard and lion (and other cats such as tiger, jaguar and puma) to one ancestor eleven million years ago. The leopard developed to have short legs, sturdy body and large skull. It is agile, able to climb trees well, swim and run at a speed approaching forty miles per hour.

Leopards are opportunistic hunters. Their natural style is to stalk their prey and will take antelopes (as large as eland), monkeys, reptiles, rodents and insects. As leopards won't defend their kill from some competitors, they prefer to take the carcass up a tree. A leopard is capable of hauling a body three times its own weight up to branches well out of reach of lions.

Territorial creatures, male leopards can have huge domains up to fifty square miles. However, females may control an area only a fifth of that size.

Leopards do meet for procreation - difficult otherwise - during the females period of heat which lasts about a week. Successful coupling will mean gestation for between ninety and one hundred and five days. Typically, there will be two or three cubs but more are not unknown. The female will find a den, perhaps in a tree hollow, a cave or rocky outcrop to give birth and for the cubs to spend their initial weeks. In Savanna, Paddy, the ranger, believed there was a young family on a rock. The excitement was enhanced by two tyre punctures. Passengers sat in the car whilst the tracker jacked up the one side and effected the change to the spare. The second time another ranger from the reserve had to loan his extra wheel. We felt vulnerable sitting with no escape and a potentially very hungry cat, needing to feed her cubs, close by. Finally, we looked around the rock. Nothing could be seen. As Paddy began to move off a small head appeared peeking over the edge. I saw it and was a hero in the car for a few seconds. Just one cub on view and only very briefly but we saw it.

There is a relatively high attrition rate for cubs. It will be a year before they can fend for themselves and even then they tend to stick close to mom for another twelve months. If the leopard survives it can live in excess of twenty years.

Chapter Two

FIRST FULL DAY

Thursday —   **Morning Drive**
Weather —   **Cool early, then fantastic**

have already described the sense of anticipation and excitement but without ever being close to expressing the surge of joy, pleasure and honour I feel at the start of another day, another adventure in the bush.

So, why is being in there better than watching on television? On TV you can see it all, closer and more graphically. Switching over to the correct channels ensures spotting every creature known to man.

Well, firstly, in the wild there is no guarantee that any animal will be seen. The rangers are very good and know typically where to find certain species. Life is unscripted, this is just more intense, more concentrated. There have been periods in which we have seen nothing. Then…wow time, something special!

Secondly, TV is two dimensional. In the wild you see, hear, smell and get a sense of scale. This doesn't mean big is good. Size doesn't matter. There is also a real perspective of speed, of distance, of volume. The depth of colours, the foreboding a roar instils and the awful stench from a carcass.

TV is fantastic for wildlife. I love it. Being there has a factor ten greater. We are extremely lucky to have done it and, truly, I know that.

Being there you can also ask questions. TV isn't interactive yet. The ranger and tracker know so much about the animals, their behaviour and the environment. There is the issue of a small threat from the killing machines on view. I think it would be difficult to guess whether the lion would be more surprised if it jumped into a car or the occupants. Uncertainty is the additional ingredient that makes it very, very special.

The weather on the first morning was fantastic. It began fresh, cool and bright and developed to wonderfully hot.

This was a classic example of us not seeing the glamorous species but having a great time. We saw no big cats, however, it was fascinating in terms of animal behaviour.

As we left the camp we immediately came across elephants, impala and giraffes. Not a bad way to begin. We were to see numerous other members of these species later on the drive. Seeing them in the vicinity of our accommodation shows how the camp is in the middle of the area inhabited by wild animals, not separate or exclusive. Animals enter the areas we occupy, usually at night because we are not evident. We scare them.

We encountered three male rhinoceroses, one of which was much larger and dominant. They were probably not related and one was much younger than his friends. They had acquired each other as browsing companions. There was no need for competition. There is plenty of foliage. Rhinos are the ultimate grass clearers. A single rhino eats 60 kilograms each day. It doesn't sleep a lot, or indeed, do anything else much. They eat.

As we watched them the rhinos watched us as best they could. They are notoriously short sighted and liable to short temper. On this occasion they were relaxed about our presence.

Male rhinos munch

In truth, rhinos are immense, imposing creatures but without much personality. These guys were in grass up to their loins. Gently, they moved forward taking a mouthful of greenery with each step. There was no urgency in the process. What is there to hurry for? It isn't a competition, there is plenty to eat at this time of the year and they fear no other animal.

In Tsavo, Kenya we did see a black rhinoceros on the move. It wasn't chasing or attacking a vehicle but something had provoked movement at pace. It is remarkable the speed they achieve, nothing short of a cannon would stop it. Grace is not a word I would have expected to use. Yet, as it accelerated on its stumpy legs the rhino seemed to become more coordinated and moved in a more compact manner. Maybe not actually graceful but harnessed power.

On one drive in the Masai Mara, the ranger asked if we wanted to see rhinoceros? He knew the answer but was polite and we may have had a driving passion to see something else at that exact moment.

There are three semi-tame rhinos in a smallish reserve, looked after by a few dedicated minders. These are fully grown animals and it was emphasised that they are not domesticated and there is always an element of risk. So, armed with a twig each the keepers ushered the huge creatures towards us. Slowly but deliberately they moved nearer. We were within ten feet of them. Nothing between us. There was a daft smile on my face which may well have provoked them had they seen it.

Could this experience have happened in Britain, in Europe or United States of America? Doubtful, because it isn't sanitised, homogenised and if something went wrong lawsuits would follow. We knew the dangers but wanted to accept the chance. Injury was highly unlikely or I wouldn't have allowed my family to stand in the open with these magnificent animals but there remained just the minor possibility. Controlled adventure.

Rhinos pictured whilst on foot

There was a large herd of elephants. Mainly females and calves, this herd had also a male in attendance. And it was in musth. His mind was on the available ladies and not as pleased to see us as we would have liked.

Tanda Tula is a super reserve in Timbavati. We were visiting in South Africa's winter. It was there we met a young bull elephant in musth. There is an odour that comes from the secretions he makes. This is an intense time for elephants. Emotions are heightened, challenges are taken on. Therefore, our arrival was perceived as unwelcome.

The ears came forward and flapped, the trunk rose and there was trumpeting to tell us we had encroached. Alison was nervous, I was probably too stupid to recognise the danger. Both the ranger and tracker waved their arms in a way that attempted to replicate a trunk moving up and down. It didn't look like it to us.

The elephant came forward and then backed off. Then forward and back stressing his anger. Eventually, he walked away. Breaking wind as he went, a recurring theme for us. Geoffrey, the ranger, accepted his right to make a final statement.

"Whatever you say, sir," said Geoffrey. The pachyderm could have flipped us over as easily as it was for him to walk into the distance. Rule one is do not try to out run an angry elephant, it won't happen. Perhaps he thought our car wasn't as well endowed as he was. Few creatures are.

It was in Timbavarti that we saw and heard the greatest number of go away birds. This is officially their name, although until recently they were known as grey lourie. It is no surprise the call of this bird clearly is "Go away". Every time we approached one it would cry, "Go away". By the

41

simple expedient of speeding up just as we got to the bird Geoffrey could make it fly away as we drove below it. All passengers would simultaneously throw arms in the air like a Mexican wave in a choreographed façade which amused us enormously. Sad.

Off to breakfast in the bush for us.

Elephants observed by Natalie in Kenya

Elephants have an unbelievable ability to disappear. They are huge, and yet, quickly, easily and quietly they vanish. Animal merging with its surroundings. It is astonishing. A few broken or chewed branches being the only evidence of tons of mobile mammal passing.

That morning, another herd of elephants was found. A female stood above us on the crest of a slope flapping her ears. Whilst she didn't come any closer, she was telling us she didn't like us. There were babies in the group.

The elephant was quite right and we left. Observation is one thing, interference is altogether very different. I re-iterate,

"Take only pictures, leave only footprints".

I described earlier the sensation opening the patio door as day breaks. This morning there had been two treats before even getting to the car.

Baboons were in the trees barking to each other. There is no doubt baboons communicate and in a sophisticated way.

Disgruntled mother elephant

Baboons de-louse

We were still out after dark. There was a real racket in the distance. Baboons were in panic. Occupying several trees a group of these primates knew there was a leopard below them. The leopard had an ambition to enjoy the delicacy baboon that night.

Artfully, the cat pretended to move away from the area. However, he looped around and hid behind our vehicle. Unintended conspiracy by us with the leopard to provide dinner in the form of a hunted baboon. I am pleased to say the baboons knew too much for the leopard and escaped into the depths of the dark bush.

Ironically, as we followed the leopard we saw it already had a dead impala carcass from which he had begun to eat the soft innards. As we watched, the leopard dragged the body up a tree and hooked the horns behind a high branch. Spread-eagled, the carcass hung in a position which appeared to show its acceptance of its place in the food chain.

"Nothing dies of old age in the wild"

Whilst not literally true, the wild is a place of violence and carnage. Elephants die of hunger. Their final set of teeth drop out and eating becomes impossible.

If impala gives a clue by having an M on its rear, the waterbuck goes even further by displaying a circular target on its bum for predators to aim for, as if they need any help.

Our second treat before the drive, drinking coffee on the veranda that morning, we saw a small herd of elegant and graceful waterbuck grazing. The animals ate just below our table on the veranda. This was a good location for them as it allowed the antelope good all round visibility, a chance to see carnivores with bad intentions. The vegetation had been cut back to help protect the lodge from fire. It also means great views for antelopes and us. As the thick vegetation had been erased it left succulent grass.

Most waterbuck spot tourists

Elephants seen from the room in Mala Mala

After the drive we had breakfast. A herd of ten elephants emerged on the opposite side of the river. It's just like living in Birmingham. An al fresco breakfast in autumn, a spectacular vista populated by exotic animals.

We went back to our room and sat on the patio. The elephants came down to the river to drink. The babies in the group replicated the style of their mothers' mannerisms. In the wild it is both nature and nurture. Elephants have a style of their own. Slow and bulky but gentle and fluid. Unique.

They stayed with us for several hours. I watched an adult female enjoy the day and the foliage. Threatened by nothing herself, her only concern was for the family. A task for the rest of her life, through a number of generations.

MAMMALS

- Baboon
- Waterbuck
- Elephant
- Impala
- Giraffe
- Tree Squirrel
- Vervet Monkey
- Kudu
- Rhinoceros

BIRDS

- Saddle-billed Stork
- Crested Francolin
- Go Away Bird
- Blacksmith Plover
- Green Spotted Dove
- Goliath Heron
- White-faced Duck
- Crowned Plover
- Red-faced Mousebird

ANIMAL OF THE CHAPTER

- Rhinoceros *(Ceratotherium simum)*

In Africa there are two species of rhinoceros, white and black. We have generally seen white rhino, which are far more common than black. Black rhino are on the verge of extinction, as are one of the sub-species of white rhino. Last year there were only four of this sub group known to be in the wild, compared with about 14,500 in total.

Rhinoceros up very close .

The name rhinoceros is based on the Greek for nose, hardly surprising given the shape of head and, on white rhinos, two horns. White is not a descriptor but a distortion of the Dutch word for wide. In fact, it is also called the square-lipped rhinoceros.

The horns are the distinguishing feature of this creature and its biggest threat. The horn is made of Keratin and is used in traditional Asian medicine, including but not only in China. This has provoked concerted poaching. One of the tactics used to protect these animals was to remove the horn under anaesthetic. In theory poachers would then have no motive to kill the individual. Good thinking, so far as it went. Unfortunately, the poachers killed the animal anyway. This ensured they wouldn't spend a great deal of time hunting down, that which to them, would be a worthless animal.

Rhinos are ungulates and herbivores. The white rhino has broad flat lips for grazing. Rhinos possess very good hearing and smell senses. The ears are shaped like pointed trumpets. However, their eyesight is poor. It would not recognise a man at thirty yards.

Other than man, rhinos only fear lions which could kill their young. Generally, the thick skin and size mean rhinos are worried about little. Males can weigh over six tons, be fourteen feet in length and six feet to the shoulder. On average the horn will grow to two feet but one was recorded at five feet long.

As the newly born calf weighs about ten stones (140 pounds) it isn't a shock that only one is born each time. Each female can repeat this every three years whilst at her peak. The gestation period is sixteen months.

White rhinos love water, including for wallowing. It is said they are solitary animals but we have observed groups on a number of occasions. As they can live for fifty years it would be a lonely existence without some level of interaction.

Daybreak

Chapter Three

FIRST FULL DAY AFTERNOON

Thursday —   **Afternoon Drive**
Weather —   **Stupendous**

The Styx Pride of lions is, in effect, an efficient killing machine. Whilst change in personnel was becoming imminent the collective efficacy won't be diminished. The dominant male was at this time thirteen years old and, as such, approaching the end of his period in control. He will be replaced by a younger fitter version of himself, possibly one of the two brothers which lived in an adjacent territory to the west of the Styx group. It was felt the brothers were edging gradually closer.

The end will come in a confrontation. This may well be gruesomely violent. At thirteen the leader of the Styx will lose. It means death - either immediately due to the severity of the wounds received in the fight or slowly as he fails to provide for himself and starves. Of course, the less he eats, the less energy he has for hunting. A vicious and accelerating cycle of decline.

Taking over a new pride the incoming male has further gracious habits. Immediately he tries to kill any young still with the pride. Extreme Darwinism in action. These are the products

51

of a failed father. If the breed is to survive it needs the fittest and strongest, the best. Whilst the lionesses may attempt to defend the progeny, the death of the cubs does make the female come into oestrous. Reward for the victor is mating time. New cubs, the product of a fit and healthy male to ensure the vigour of the pride. And he now has servants who will do all the hunting for him until he is usurped as he inevitably will be. The only question is when?

It is believed the females do have other "tricks". For example, a pregnant lioness may copulate with the new leader to convince him that any unborn cubs are his. In a complete reversal of this there is evidence of spontaneous abortion occurring. Again, this would bring on oestrous and a new cycle.

Elderly male lion waiting for the ladies to catch supper

Matriarch lion completely unbothered by us

On this evening we found the pride just after dark. They had purpose and intent. The male was, as ever, leading from the rear. It was very evident as they moved forward strongly that the ageing process was catching up with the old man. Scrawny and unimpressive, no aspiring royalty was going to be deterred.

Tonight, courtesy of a younger female lion, we saw a steenbok. Only moments before we found them this little antelope had been alert, precise in its features and thriving. Now it sagged in the shape of a shallow arch from the mouth of a successful predator. If there was any good news it was that it was already dead. There were no late stirrings or further feline action to conclude this young life. We were saved the agony of seeing its final seconds. It is natural and necessary but I don't need to see it. I love living animals. I am an emotional vegetarian.

It wasn't good; it wasn't bad; it was fact.

53

A lovely lady in our vehicle (Jan Earl who was with her husband Richard) was quite distressed at just seeing a dead animal, so we didn't watch for long. The sight, smell and sounds as the lion tore the carcass apart, crunched the slender bones and punctured the inflated innards of its capture were graphic enough.

It was surprising the other members of the pride did not come to share this small meal. How did they know it was a Meal for One? Could they tell from the steenbok's cry at the moment of its ultimate capitulation? Or do lions communicate? It is believed lions make around fifty distinct sounds. More and more research is showing the higher levels of intelligence animals possess. Increasingly, we are establishing different creatures feel emotions. Many of us are not amazed at all by this.

A mix of generations of lions

The line of lions stretched over fifty yards. The group was made up of lionesses and their cubs. They moved with obvious intent. As it was now two hours after daybreak it was more likely the cats were off to rest in a favourite spot where there would be some respite from

the heat of the day. Even animals which have evolved over tens of thousands of years to live in this environment cannot ignore the extremes of the weather. It may be perfect for tourists but twelve hours of non-stop sunshine is a problem to all creatures.

After the main group had passed us we noticed a single female well behind the rest. Whilst she looked thoroughly healthy she seemed distracted and agitated. She had a small difficulty or, more accurately, three small difficulties - cubs. These were cubs with a different aim to mom. The mother wanted to follow the family to shelter. The babies wanted to play. So, mom picked up one carried it twenty yards put it down and went back to fetch the next one. And so on. A cunning process only undermined by the cubs refusing to remain where they were put. More often than not the deposited youngster would follow its mother back to its sibling. The mother turned each time in exasperation to see the previous package only feet behind her. It was slow progress. Did the little ones care? No, it even appeared a deliberate attempt to miff her. Children will be children whatever the species.

Boys will be boys even if mom does impose herself

55

Eventually a semblance of order was constructed and a short line of short lions headed for the pride. Rarely have we seen anything as cute. It is inevitable my interpretation of animal behaviour is set against a comparison with human characteristics and, therefore, potentially inappropriate but there were definite similarities with naughty children. A combination of inquisitive and wilful, excess energy and a desire to keep the parental protection close.

Of course, we complicated our observation by applying a blanket of our emotions and characteristics. We know steenboks mate for life and the female partner would be close by waiting for her ex-mate. This added another dimension to our perspectives of this minor drama in the broader life in the bush. Would she grieve? Would she live for long without him? Could she find another mate? Or did she just get on with being a ruminant until her day in the jaws of a hungry carnivore?

Earlier in the afternoon we had re-visited the female leopard with the impala kill. No emotion necessary here. The antelope was long since dead, leopards are beautiful and there was only half of a carcass remaining anyway. The leopard was a few feet away from the meat but she was still guarding it even though she was not actually aware her sister was just one hundred yards to the east. Now totally independent there is no sibling affiliation. A meeting would be highly charged. The second sister would have known about the kill from the stench. Indeed, anything within a mile could not have helped but be aware. Perhaps television does have advantages.

In hope, Sister II moved closer. She could not know which other creature had the prize. The potential adversary could have been a lion. Then the next step would be Animal Heaven just before the steenbok. So, she retreated as quietly as she had approached.

Mud, mud, glorious mud

We could perceive graphically how the sisters would be competing for territory and, as this was traditionally her area, with their mother. Mother is known as the Campbell Koppie Leopard. Mala Mala camp name the animals according to the geographical domain. So, a leopard we had seen the previous evening is the "Bicycle Crossing Leopard". Literally his area includes a ford across the River Sand used by local people on bikes. Naturally, once a male leopard was in residence it became a crossing once used by bicycles. A shame it wasn't renamed the "Crossing Previously Used by Bicycles Leopard". A train of thought which pursued would lead to madness.

For a herd of eight adult and four young elephants the waterhole had obvious attractions. They drank by the gallon and then took more. This is one of those sights we have all seen on television. The elephant inserts its trunk into the water, then curls it to squirt the liquid into its mouth in classical elephant behaviour.

This place had something better, a mud bath. There is nothing to beat mud to cool the body. Young and old alike bathed. However, it was clear for the mothers it was healthy therapy but for their children it was a game; it was play time. All kids love to get dirty and this was with parental permission. Does that make it even more fun or take the edge of it? Whatever, to wallow is to give joy to the watching punters.

There is the constant conundrum, how long do we watch these beautiful animals having fun before we go in search of another exciting sight? Will the next animal show us different things, extreme behaviour? An elephant in the hand or a leopard in the bush? We remained in wonder for just thirty minutes and then the elephants began to move. Our cue to seek alternatives. There are always animals to see but which ones today?

Nothing quite like it for cooling the blood

Chameleon found at night! One of Alison's great encounters with nature

Real excitement occurred yards from the camp as a genet cat was (very) briefly spotted. Not actually a cat but a member of the family Viverridae, along with civet and mongoose. It is a very timid creature, nocturnal and well camouflaged, so a brilliant spot by Marka, in the dark. Not a glamorous animal but its rarity gave us a buzz.

In the distance we saw a few flashes of lightning. By the time we finished dinner it was a light show which transformed night into day. At 11.30 pm it began to rain. The thunder could have penetrated the consciousness of a stone deaf eighty year old who was wearing headphones through which Wagner was being played at full volume. Or to put it another way it was very loud. Our sleep was disturbed but still the alarm call was due at 5.30 am. Alison would have been dreaming of her most recent encounter with nature. Despite night having fallen a chameleon had been espied. Andrew picked it off a branch.

Not surprisingly, the little reptile was nervous but it climbed onto Alison's arm. Again, not massive in the greater scheme of things; Alison was thrilled.

Kenya spans the Equator. So, this was our first ever journey into the Southern Hemisphere.

Our lodge on the first evening was called Ngulia, in Tsavo West . I will admit to a degree of nervousness at sleeping on safari. I had no idea what it would be like, no point of reference. In reality the rooms were functional, pleasant and seemed to be snake proof.

By the time we arrived the nine of us in the car were tired and grubby. The journey had been long. From Mombasa to the entrance to the park is 250 kilometres. Then, thankfully, we had been able to drive around for nearly two hours in the reserve.

Remembering this was our first experience everything thrilled us. A baboon was at the entry gate, washing his unmentionables. Not a cuddling opportunity. Sprinting gazelles were awesome. The most spectacular sight on this leg of the trip was just outside of Ngulia.

Maribou stork in Tsavo, Kenya

A very large male elephant was above us at the edge of a rock face. He stood, ears forward and spread out, his whole body rocking back and forth. He gave no impression of goodwill. Magnificent.

Despite our physical state we wanted to explore and have a drink. The bar and dining area were strategically placed to allow the visitors to watch the waterhole by which the lodge had been built. Yet, there was just a five feet wall for a cat to climb to join us for a beer. Again, inexperience gave rise to internal butterflies but, of course, it's absolutely fine.

An elephant strolled in for a drink. Just like that. We were amazed and really excited. A maribou stork stood motionless to one side. Even this sight was great. It was all new. Little did we know it was a carrion eater and as vile in its habits as a vulture. At dusk he took off, did a large circle and departed. It held us spellbound.

We returned to the bar early in hope of more sightings. The lodge's party trick was the placement of an animal carcass in the tree next to the waterhole. A local leopard sometimes would visit for easy pickings. To our great disappointment no leopard came. There is a problem here for me. Whilst this is great customer service it fails two tests;

- it is not natural, which is my desire. Back to the television or a zoo if all you want to do is see an animal

- if a creature becomes reliant on gifts it may lose its ability to fend for itself. If attitudes or people change and, therefore, the meat isn't provided, for the leopard in this case, it could mean it cannot adapt back to its natural behaviour. Some years ago we were in the Maldives and the main excitement was a twice weekly feeding of stingrays. One of the staff brought a bucket of food to a specific spot. He would then hand feed half-a-dozen of these fish. In fact, the rays would even pick the man's pockets for food and jump into the bucket. Great entertainment but the caveats apply. Indeed, the rays came everyday but only received food occasionally. And if it stops?

We saw little that evening, although a hyena walked through the edge of the area lit up by the lights of the lodge.

As I got into bed there was a loud noise outside my window. An elephant and the hyena from dinner had a small spat within feet of my room. Good grief.

The next day we set off to Tsavo East. The day was gorgeous, and memorable for visiting two places.

My favourite sign is at Mzemi Springs in Kenya.

A young Nat in a hat by a slightly worrying sign

So, if you die it is your problem. I loved the emphasis that you are LIKELY to bump into hippos, crocodiles and..? However, please proceed quietly, presumably to ensure dozing animals can sleep soundly.

The group in front of us had a guard with a rifle. Where was our man with a gun? We braved it without armoury. A narrow path wound round to the pools. Six feet from the water edge there was another sign, " Do not go past here". Some chance. I wasn't getting off the path because wild animals know they cannot come on the slabs, the mud is for them.

The Mzima Springs are really two pools below the Chyulu Hills. The word Mzima means "alive". It lives because of the 50 million gallons of fresh water that flows into the pools every day. It is alive with fish and birds as well as hippos and crocs. It is alive with the tour bus atmosphere of a very popular stopping spot in Tsavo West.

On this occasion in the water were about a dozen hippos. Grunting and lurching, they appeared occupied. This was good news as there was nothing to stop them joining us on land. Or, indeed, the sunbathing crocodile. This was our first real experience of open contact with deadly creatures. Getting back to the car we were all very chipper about our bravery and the true spirit of adventure we had just shown. Next stage is to train to be a ranger.

As we drove up a road which, in truth, was very unattractive, we turned a bend at the top of a hill and directly in front of us was the magnificent view of Mount Kilimanjaro, "Shining Mountain." We looked across Tanzania to the highest mountain in Africa, a dormant volcano. Note, not dead but sleeping. It is 5,895m high, which is 19,330 feet. As the weather was so good there was a fantastic open view. Two thirds of the way up there was a ring of cloud but it was quite shallow and we could see the mountain top which was amazingly flat with a smooth rounded ice-cap. It is the natural that thrills.

It is fascinating to note the estimate is Kilimanjaro was formed one million years ago. Yet Kenya is the site of the earliest evidence of man, perhaps dating back four million years. Therefore, man would have seen the eruption. Presumably, this is the Garden of Eden.

The waterhole at Voi

We were out all day. The two reserves of West and East Tsavo combine to be one of the largest in the world. They cover an area greater than the size of Wales. So we meandered our way to the next lodge. We saw many herbivores but no cats. A dramatic sight was a running herd of buffalo but they hadn't been spooked by a lion or two. We kept, as we should, to the roads and saw only those animals which came our way.

The Voi Lodge in East Tsavo has a completely different position. It is situated on top of a cliff, which overlooks a waterhole. From my room I could watch the lines of animals arrive for vital sustenance. There seemed to a pecking order. Elephants first, zebra next, followed by wildebeest and so on. Who decides?

This is the venue for Alison's baboon story. Baboons abound at Voi. They have a free run of the place; like they could be stopped short of a cull. As ever I was in a separate room. We had just arrived and instead of shutting the outside door my wife and daughter went about their activities thoughtlessly. This meant the bathroom for Natty, again with the door open, so she watched the adult male baboon stroll into the room. Finally showing some nous Natty slammed the door shut. This left Alison face-to-face with an innately aggressive primate. Who was more surprised? Alison grabbed for her camera, which startled the baboon, he leapt towards her, snarled and ran out wetting himself on the only item of my clothing in their room, a sweatshirt. I was called to administer wisdom, "You're a pair of prats". Alison went to reception where a nice lady told her she should keep the door closed. Brilliant advice. However, a member of staff did come to clear the mess. Nobody offered to wash the sweatshirt and I wasn't carrying the stench around for two days, so it went in the bin. Shame, it was a nice sweater.

Voi Lodge has a swimming pool. Why? Some children were playing in it, really spoiling the atmosphere. Bah, humbug. We explored. There was another sign near the edge of the ridge, "Do not pass this point". I don't need telling twice. Was it the chance of falling off the edge? Apparently not. People (which people?) said it was because of the snakes. Yikes, keep well away.

Randomly appearing around Voi were some of the cutest creatures we have seen - hyrax. These rodents have no limits, they browse wherever they find foliage primarily in rocky areas. Voi is perfect, as it is built on a rock face and tourists are always dropping food, to be scooped up by these little herbivores. Hyrax are also known as shrewmouse and rockbadger and resemble a well fed rabbit with short ears. It is a delight to open the door of the accommodation to find an inquisitive fur ball looking at you hopefully. I am not sure picking up a hyrax for a cuddle would be a good idea. Aside from the unlikely event one could be caught, the teeth and claws look sharp.

It was possible to get near to the waterhole by walking down steps to a tunnel which then inched out towards the animals. The tunnel was small and dark. Snakes? Paranoia rules. Actually, we saw nothing at all.

Food that evening was great but there were to be no nocturnal animal encounters.

Next morning I was awake very early, like the little boy I am really. How lucky I was. Walking adjacent to the waterhole was a family of meerkats. I only saw them for a few minutes but it was fascinating. They really do have guards out at the four points. Guards stand up, check it is safe and the group move forward. Repeat process time and again. No one else was yet up because our departure wasn't until quite late. This misses the point of safari big time.

Mr Hassan was very keen to find a big cat. So, we drove miles and miles. He was presuming the lack of a lion, leopard or cheetah could affect his tip. This situation was aggravated by his inability to answer many questions; and we had many. We had given up hope and were on the way to exit gate when I (that's me) saw a shape and some movement. I was sure I knew what it was. I've seen the documentaries. Lion.

I shouted, "stop". We did, instantly. Everyone was on their feet. Would it emerge from the bush? The others were manic and my credibility was on the line. Well, I wouldn't be telling the story if I had

Our only lion in Tsavo

been wrong. A single, fairly tatty lioness strolled across the road. Our vow of temperate behaviour went for a moment. Two days and we had seen a lion. Showing our naiveté we held the pop-up roof on the car in case the lion jumped at us and we could then slam it down, safe.

Mr Hassan told us he knew he would find us a lion. Indeed.

MAMMALS
- Bushbuck
- Kudu
- Waterbuck
- Grey Duiker
- Impala
- Elephant
- Giraffe
- Zebra
- Leopard
- Lion *Styx Pride*
- Steenbok
- Genet Cat
- Slender Mongoose

REPTILE
- Chameleon

BIRDS
- Tambourine Dove
- Egyptian Goose
- Blackwinged Plover
- Bateleur
- Spotted Eagle Owl

ANIMAL OF THE CHAPTER

■ Lion *(Panthera leo)*

Magnificent and dominant

Lions differ from other cats in that they are social animals, living and hunting together. Whilst the average size of a pride is about six some are much larger. In Masai Mara we knew there was a group called the Marsh Pride. Heavily featured on the television's Big Cat Diary, this is a superb hunting consortium. All prides consist of one or two dominant males, lionesses related to each other and their offspring. The women do the work; they bring up the children; they do the hunting.

The Marsh Pride consisted of more than thirty members when we saw them. It appeared to be a very healthy group, as well. There were numerous cubs, of various ages. Children play, including these boys and girls. Dad didn't join in.

There is a high attrition rate amongst cubs. A litter will usually be one to four cubs and many other species try to kill them young, before they reach maturity when they are safer. Buffalo, hyenas, jackal, leopards, crocodiles all see cubs as fair game, if mother, aunties and granny are not in the vicinity. Then, of course, there is man. If, as has happened, lions decide man is a tasty treat, the lion(s) need to be killed. However, lions are only safe from man in the reserves, and then if the guardians are watching for poachers.

Lions may become man eaters because of tooth decay or illness or if the usual prey are becoming difficult to find. The normal diet is ungulates, such as buffalo, zebra, gazelles and other antelope but especially wildebeest and impala.

Males are ejected from the pride when maturity is reached. This reduces conflict with the dominant male, probably dad, and interbreeding. Frequently, young males will form a group, especially to aid hunting. The most visible difference between the sexes is the mane around the head and neck of the male. The bigger and darker the mane, the more likely a female will want him. It shows other males he is a testosterone filled fighting and loving machine.

A male of the species may weigh a quarter of a ton, be half as big again as a female and, if he stood on his rear feet, tower by three feet above a man. Its canine teeth can be three inches long. Lions will also scavenge, taking a kill off a leopard for instance.

The female will begin producing from about four years of age and has a gestation period of three and a half months. She may live in the wild for twenty years. A male is unlikely to exceed eight years but we saw one who was thirteen. In captivity both will live longer before dying of boredom.

Wildebeest and zebras drink in the Mara

Chapter Four

FRIDAY MORNING

Friday —   **Morning Drive**
Weather —   **Wet and Cool**

I talked earlier of the trainspotting style of safari — see it, photograph it, tick a box, move on to the next one. Our mentality is different. The extra joy comes from seeing the animals display behaviour beyond sleeping, eating and walking.

The two sister leopards were again in close proximity. This time the second sister was lying in long grass but sister one was up a tree, lounging spreadeagled along a branch. The residue of the long dead impala was protruding from behind the trunk of the tree. The reason sister one had withdrawn to 15 feet above ground came by almost immediately. A family of mother and three adolescent hyena were interested in the odour of meat. The smell of the half eaten impala was compelling. Hyenas would kill the leopard. So, the only way to survive and keep the carcass was for sister one to retreat to an appropriate height. She could easily stay up the tree all day. Food still available and she is less concerned about using a recently sanitised toilet. No worries from hyena.

71

Leopard sister one

Leopard sister two

Sister two had moved to the base of a different tree. She lay observing life but ready for a rapid climb to an available branch. Hyenas are genetically linked to cats but cannot climb trees. They join vultures and crocodiles in the "Why do they exist?" category. Detestable (except their cute babies) and grasping, hyenas are so strong and violent that lions won't take on a pack of them. These creatures perform a fundamental role in the complex food chain, they are critical to the health of the bush and aesthetics aren't everything. However, we ascribe human characteristics to them and then they don't seem very attractive. They eat anything, sometimes beginning before their victim is dead, prefer to wait for others to do the killing, look ugly and particularly like to eat cute little babies of other species. Not nice.

At the other end of the Ahhh! Spectrum are grey duikers. Small and exact of feature, timid and graceful, these animals bounce like a tennis ball with four legs and huge eyes. If you get near to one it will only be for an instant as they trust no-one and nothing.

During this drive we saw four of the big five. Also, I missed two fleeing hippos as I was photographing a small herd of nyala. The hippos were in a pool but sped back to the safety of the river and effective invisibility. On a drive it is not possible to see everything. I am certain animals deliberately pop out after we pass and laugh.

The rain overnight had transformed the landscape. In six hours there had been a true deluge of precipitation. The River Sand was in full flow and was going to increase as the waters which fell in the hills worked their way down stream. Fords were barely passable, the vehicles inched their way across the river adding another level of threat. This is a waterway with hippos and crocodiles - not for swimming by me.

Elephants have developed a clever ploy of meshing small branches and leaves to create an umbrella. Memorable.

Buffalo with adornment

In the first two and a half hours we saw many animals, particularly an abundance of impala and a plethora of giraffe. In the final hour we saw a babbling family of baboons, a buffalo strolling with a twig behind his ear, an elephant posing for photographs and the annoyance of hyenas with the leopard sisters.

This was a really special outing. We got a little wet and breakfast tasted even better than ever.

The time between drives allows the punters to pursue several options. The most popular is sleep, catching up the lost hours of the night. Many people read and relax. Most camps have a swimming pool. At Savanna, Alison chose to lie by the pool with a book. Perfectly pleasant and no apparent problems.

A day later Alison noticed a lump on her leg. It grew over the next few days, became redder and itched. The staff correctly declared it was a spider bite. However, as it grew the wisdom in our party "confirmed" it was snake bite and finally shark bite. We were home before she went to the doctors. A simple course of antibiotics the remedy. Thankfully, the nasty insect did not lay its eggs in Alison's leg, an activity not unknown. These little perishers get everywhere. Each morning I bang my boots on the floor and shake my clothes to remove any unwanted guests. Spiders, scorpions and snakes do not ask permission prior to residency and take umbrage if the owner puts a foot into the now occupied shoe.

The two nights before we went to Sabi Sands we stayed at the Rissington Inn in Hazyview. Mary Minett's shoe became home to a frog. The world heard about it very quickly as a cry of anguish was emitted. Not withstanding the Rissington was a restful place and gave us the chance to explore the area and, especially, the Blyde River Canyon. The most spectacular view was from God's Window. The valley below is several thousand feet down. As cloud can fill the void that is the valley we counted ourselves very lucky to have such a great view - not a Hazyview at all.

My knees shook and were a bit weak from the height and the construction of the platform to protrude out over the colossal drop. It cannot last forever, so when will it fall?

It was here I bought the Rhino Repelling Stick. Amongst the best ten Rand any man has ever spent.

MAMMALS
- Grey Duiker
- Impala
- Rhinoceros
- Nyala
- Hippopotamus

- Giraffe
- Kudu
- Zebra
- Baboon
- Tree Squirrel
- Buffalo
- Elephant
- Leopard
- Hyena

BIRDS

- Three-banded Plover
- Waxbill
- Little Bee-eater
- Arrow-marked Babbler
- Wire-tailed Swallow

ANIMAL OF THE CHAPTER

- Elephant *(Loxodonta africana)*

Elephants in Tanda Tula

The largest land animal, often weighing seven tons and even ten tons has been recorded. Elephants are grey and imposing with three specific differentiators;

A trunk - a combination of nose and upper lip which has evolved to be a flexible hand as well.

Two tusks - made of ivory these are the incisors, the only teeth not to be constantly renewed through life. The longest reached ten feet. It is these tusks that make the elephant subject to man's cruelty; ivory is valuable. So, in come the poachers, backed by middlemen who make a bigger profit.

Large flat ears - even bigger on the African elephant than its Indian relatives.

Elephants are herbivores which eat all day and a large proportion of the night. In effect, they are both diurnal and nocturnal. Females live in herds which have been known to have two hundred members led by a matriarch. It won't have mature males, which will live in bachelor herds.

Like the rhino, elephants have poor eyesight but unlike rhinos they also have poor hearing (despite huge ear flaps).

Giraffe awaits his turn as an elephant drinks

Elephants, through their large trunk, do have excellent smelling capabilities.

Elephants love water for sustenance, cleaning, wallowing and swimming, using the trunk as a snorkel.

Oestrus begins when a female is about thirteen. A calf can weigh eighteen stones and there are cases of twins. Gestation lasts twenty two months - so the loss of any animal impacts on the viability of the species.

If elephants die naturally their life span can be over sixty five years. Memory is traditionally the facility for which elephants are best known. The more we know, the more research undertaken, the more this seems correct. Generations pass on knowledge of waterholes, best feeding grounds and directions.

Chapter Five

FRIDAY AFTERNOON

Friday –	**Afternoon Drive**
Weather –	**Grey and overcast**

This was a relatively quiet drive in grey, oppressive weather. However, no outing is ever without interest. This was our fifth drive and yet we saw four new mammals, two of which I had never seen before anywhere.

The klipspringer was sat on top of a rocky outcrop, eleven feet high. Petite and delicate this antelope has fantastic agility. Even more impressive than its fleet footed descent to terra firma was its ascent back up again. It does it more easily than many creatures travel on flat ground. Nimble is its middle name. The ability to climb is obviously a great escape route from potential predators.

Another solitary antelope was a steenbok. Technically, we had already seen one but it was dead and hanging from both sides of a lioness' mouth. This one was alert and perky. Ears pricked it wasn't sure if a Land Rover was dangerous or not. The answer is, of course, it depends who is driving. On this occasion it was just people who wanted to shoot pictures. Cameras are only threatening when operated by private detectives and the paparazzi.

Klipspringer has sprung

Whilst it is not a coincidence that nearly everyone we have met in the wild is similarly interested in the animals and the country but they have all been charming and great company as well. We also met two well known naturalists, briefly.

Jonathan Scott is perhaps best known for his work on the BBC's "Big Cat Diary", centred on the Masai Mara during the migration period. Of course, his CV is extremely extensive but television highlights and priorities for the viewer, so he is now recognised primarily for that programme. We had booked through a package based on Big Cat Diary, which included a talk from Jonathan. Indeed, that is how it happened but I remain unconvinced he was aware of the commitments which had been made on his behalf. Not withstanding it was a fascinating couple of hours. Particularly helpful were the tips for improving our photography and as only we were booked on this trip we did have personal attention.

Over dinner it became clear Jonathan Scott is a dedicated professional with sound principles and an acute sense of the issues facing us. His interests go far beyond Kenya. He is also justifiably proud of his family.

The most often shown footage involving Jonathan Scott starred a cheetah named Kike. This is a remarkable lady with a unique habit. All cheetahs use elevated points to assist their hunting and Kike sees 4x4 vehicles as mobile hills. She jumps onto the cars to gain a better perspective of potential prey. On the memorable day filmed for Big Cat Diary, Kike was on the Land Rover in which Scott was sat. As he talked to camera Kike did that which is natural; she urinated, on the television presenter's head. He had the decency to laugh at himself. On one trip to Kenya we almost had the unbridled thrill of Kike climbing onto our vehicle. In the end, she leapt onto the car next to us. Brilliant for photography but it was so close to it being our car and our close up experience. The people in the lucky car didn't seem too sure this was a blessing.

Kike in classic pose

Arriving for the safari in Timbavati we were asked to share a car on the short journey to the Tanda Tula camp. The other person was Ian Douglas-Hamilton, again a naturalist with an immense reputation, particularly for his work with elephants. Television now has cast him more famously as the father of Saba Douglas-Hamilton, who also works on Big Cat Diary. Ian was speaking at a conference at the camp. We shared the reverse journey as well but it was not long enough to even slightly tap into the knowledge and stories he has to relate.

Warthogs and hoglets

See any animal and stop the car. Warthogs are cute, so a pair was worth viewing. But better were the three youngsters - Hoglets. All baby creatures have charm. These had it in spades. It is a wonderfully comic sight as the hoglets ran along with their aerial tails erect. How do they survive in a land populated by lions and leopards? Maybe they would merely be a snack not worthy of too much effort and energy. Warthogs dig tunnels to escape and avoid danger - a good plan generally but there is film of a pride of lions systematically digging into the hole and dragging out the warthog for consumption. The lions had a rota, shared the work and then fought for the spoils. Definitely a further example of communication and sophisticated behaviour, combined with hierarchical and base instinct.

A bull of a male leopard was lying deep in a wooded outcrop near Londolozi, as big as we had ever seen. It seemed unlikely he would be on the move soon. As ever rangers were politely waiting their turn, moving in and staying just a short while, then allowing others to look. This was the only occasion, in our experience, that a fellow passenger behaved rudely. This man was impatient and obnoxious. Forget the queue, he wanted to see the leopard. He was only with us for one drive. I suspect the ranger quietly moved him to another vehicle.

Superb male leopard by which we walked later

As we reversed from the spot, we almost ran over a warthog. This was a fully grown male. Comically, his head protruded from his hole. It resembled a trophy head hunters would put on the wall. We could see nothing else and with the leopard feet away he had no intention of revealing any more. This was one very nervous pig.

Later that morning I joined an organised walk. We strolled around a large pool from which a family of hippopotamus watched (as well as they can) our progress. As ever there was no barrier to the whole tribe tagging along. If this made me nervous then a detour to within twenty yards of the leopard's place of repose made me sweat. No harm done but when I mentioned it to Sandos our driver it stirred him to rush off to give graphic guidance to his colleague who had led our perilous meander.

In most game parks there is a mid-drive break. In the evening this is for a Sundowner - a beer, coffee or gin. Coffee for me then (perhaps). This is also a chance to use the toilet facilities. Choose your bush, check for alien bodies which have already taken up residence. The idea of being bitten or stung is repellent, the idea of being bitten or stung in a sensitive area is cold sweat frightening. Every tree is a lavatree - "Boom, boom," a fox once said.

April is early autumn in the Southern Hemisphere, so the temperature does drop towards darkness. Driving along in an open vehicle allows the accentuating aspect of wind. It can become chilly. The answer is layers. In the morning as the day warms it is easy to peel off and reverse the process in the evening.

As the drive continued after dark, the headlights and searchlight kept us in the "hunt". However, shadows create shapes and shapes translate into exciting…trees. A log becomes an impala; a tree is an elephant.

When an elephant did appear it was highly imposing. Being grey anyway, it assumed the physical characteristics of a gargantuan phantom. Half real, half ghost, each elephant fills your vision and stirs the soul. Can anything be this unreal and actual in one entity?

Almost as spooky was the totally immobile giant eagle owl. It was sat in a tree looking down (in every regard) on us. Two feet of pure malice but beautiful in a macabre way. Rodents beware.

MAMMALS
- Waterbuck (in the camp)
- Nyala (in the camp)
- Impala
- Zebra
- Wart Hog and "hoglets"
- Elephant
- Klipspringer
- Steenbok
- Black Backed Jackal
- Wildebeest
- Kudu

REPTILES
- Terrapin
- Nile Monitor

BIRDS
- European Bee-eater
- Green-backed Heron
- Greater Blue-eared Glossy Starling
- Barn Swallow
- Grey Heron
- Giant Eagle Owl
- Harlequin Quail

ANIMAL OF THE CHAPTER

■ Cheetah *(Acinonyx jubata)*

Famously, the fastest land animal in the world. I love cheetahs for their exquisite features, their vulnerability and their resolve. It is very difficult for cheetah cubs to reach maturity. The problems are numerous, predators abound and the species is under threat. The first cheetah we encountered was in South Africa, sitting quietly after feeding. Ironically, we have only seen cheetah in Kenya since then.

Top speed is achieved in three seconds, as the cheetah runs at up to seventy five miles per hour to catch its prey. Only a percentage of chases are successful and then the kill is subject to other predators snatching it away. Some cheetahs are 50% successful at their prime. It cannot repel lions, leopards or hyenas as it is smaller and slight. Weighing a maximum 40 pounds, it can be four feet long and three feet tall. Not big compared the other predators.

Three cheetah brothers

Cheetah mom and cubs

Cheetahs are different from other big cats in that they hunt during the day, as they track by sight rather than smell, so light is needed. Females live solitary lives except when they have cubs but males often join one or two others, frequently their brothers. Indeed, we saw three brothers together.

Litters of cubs can number six or seven after a gestation period of three months. Only through mass delivery can a female have a realistic chance of getting any to maturity. Typically, a mature cheetah will live to just twelve years old - this is a creature under threat.

Only one tusk elephant

Chapter Six

SATURDAY MORNING

Saturday — **Morning**
Weather — **Back to beautiful**

Generally, this was a trip of solitary animals or very small groups. Whilst we also saw a large family of irritated baboons and a herd of impala near to camp, it was mainly individual animals to observe.

For the first time we saw members of the Eyrefield pride of lions. There were three lionesses, different generations with a similar objective - finding food. They were clearly interested in a hunt, yet when we encountered them a grey duiker was only fifty yards away and ignored. This may be because it would constitute little more than elevenses to a fully grown lion and the girls wanted a full South African breakfast. It wasn't worth the effort.

The lions of the Eyrefield pride are larger than the Styx family and appeared to have a greater sense of menace. We were fortunate enough to find them as the sun rose. This allowed us to have a splendid view of the array of subtle colours in their coats. Each different but an inherent gold hue which makes them the special one in the bush.

Ladies of the Eyrefield pride

Mala Mala is attached to the Kruger National Park and there is no fence between them. As we were taken along next to the park there were three giraffes browsing gently in the trees. Our ranger could not approach to look more closely, as he cannot cross the border. Rightly, he has to respect the provenance of the authorities. This is not a world in which rules and laws can be ignored. It would be very dangerous without discipline and standards and, furthermore, they must be maintained as a message to poachers and others who do not respect the environment and the lives of the wonderful animals. These pockets of excellence should be used as the foundation for the messages to be spread widely. It is only one part of the answer but the value must not be underestimated.

In Kenya the Wildlife Service has produced *The Wildlife Code.*
The relevant sections are;

- **Do not harass the wildlife.** *Making a noise, flashing lights and sudden movements can frighten the animals and makes them aggressive towards humans. Especially when game viewing keep quiet.*

- **Do not drive off the road** *where there is an existing road system. Vehicles leaving the road damage the habitat and can alter drainage patterns.*

- **Do not discard litter**
  food or cigarette butts - fire can cause enormous damage to vegetation and kills wildlife which cannot escape.

- **Do show consideration** *for the animals you are watching, and to other wildlife enthusiasts. Ensure that animals are not completely surrounded by vehicles.*

- **Do keep to the 40km/h speed limit** *and drive carefully.*

- **Do not leave your car.** *For your own safety, only get out of your car at designated picnic sites and nature trails. In case of a breakdown, it is best to wait for help, so always carry water and extra food.*

- **Do not feed the animals -** *remember they are wild. Monkeys and baboons can be a nuisance searching for food.*

- **Do remember wild animals can be dangerous.** *Unless you have adequate protection and are supervised by a professional guide, do not stand up in your vehicle.*

- *Do not remove flora and fauna.*

- *Do not enter or leave a park except through the authorised park gates.*

Savannah is the landscape between desert and forest. At times it is arid and coarse but in the wet season becomes lush. It doesn't only occur in Africa but worldwide in Tropical and Sub Tropical areas. The woodland is denser at different points, the grass higher and the scrub less passable. Some of the trees are prolific; the acacia, eucalyptus and baobab are particularly well known. This is perfect for browsing and grazing animals.

Sitting by some giraffes but scanning the horizon I spotted a buffalo through my binoculars. I was proud of my excellent spot of one of the big five. We set off to get a better view. Slightly embarrassingly, it was a solitary wildebeest. In my defence;

1. Buffalo are often found alone

2. Previously, the wildebeest we have seen have been in colossal herds

3. They are both dark skinned and have horns

4. I wanted it to be a buffalo

Ho hum…

It seemed more poignant when it was a single wildebeest. As a good meal for lions this animal must have been highly vulnerable. There is no possibility of safety from the Flotilla Principle i.e. get into the middle of the herd and let another individual make the ultimate sacrifice. In fact, the wildebeest had joined up with a couple of zebra. He probably thought he was a zebra and had rubbed off the stripes in a mud bath. Mating could be a surprise to one or both participants.

Gnu and zebra share grassland

A million hours of film have been committed to "crossings" of the Mara River. As the ruminants move to and from the Serengeti in search of food they must cross the river. There are numerous points at which this happens; the only constant is the presence of crocodiles. These are the biggest fodder opportunities of the year. There is no subtlety to this process, the crocs lie openly in wait. The wildebeest and zebra know they have to traverse the river and that the croc wants them.

Our good fortune has been to see an actual crossing twice. These were the result of a number of hours sat watching the herbivores prevaricate about the value of leaping into the water here and now. Groups would walk to the water edge, look at the crocodile, think better of it and retreat back to the main herd. Then more would come down and repeat the process. And again; and again.

Preparing for the plunge to cross the Mara

Giraffes would intersperse zebras and wildebeest, and then go back up the bank. After all, they can graze anywhere, so don't need to enter the water.

So, back and forth, back and forth - then a large wildebeest went for it. Why that moment? There was no clue but in he went. Up came the crocodile with mouth open wide enough to take out an animal ten times its own size. But, thankfully, also into the water went scores of other wildebeest. The crocodile disappeared, not to be seen again. I don't know if it was killed or it merely retreated but an estimated five hundred animals got over safely.

It was thrilling for us and satisfying to see the good guys win on this occasion. The only disappointment was the tourist mass (including us) surrounding this miracle of the wild. Lines of vehicles with cameras whirring and people giggling.

It was also gratifying that we didn't observe any animals injure themselves or each other in their single-minded approach to crossing. If one falls the others drive on, which does, at times, mean trampling members of their own species.

They are in the water

The other time we saw this event was incomplete. The crossing had already begun but we did see a stream of animals run across the water for nearly half-an-hour. Once out of the river the wildebeests kept running for a few seconds but zebras stopped as soon as they got to the top of the new bank. A number of them brayed in celebration and relief. There is no doubt it was an expression of emotion.

There was no obvious reason the procession ceased as it did, why thousands safely crossed but many thousands more bottled it. This time the crocodiles had taken out a large male wildebeest. The carcass was lying in the river, semi-submerged for consumption later. Sad but inevitable in the food chain.

The depth of the water was very shallow at this point. The logic of using this location was clear. Why some zebras re-crossed is less so. Bravado or stupidity? My money is on crass idiocy. These are animals prey to the most vicious killers in the wild and they have black and white stripes. It isn't the best camouflage but the species continues to thrive.

Close to camp a young male elephant was progressing through a succulent tree, near to a pair of foraging warthogs. Excepting their own species on occasions, herbivores don't bother about each other. Let's be honest there are enough carnivores around to consider.

The overnight weather forecast had been for cloudy conditions but dry. As we had opened the curtain at 5.30 am we noticed two things;

- a complete lack of cloud. It was to be an exceptional day.
- baboons around the pool. This is, indeed, civilised living.

MAMMALS
- Baboon
- Lions *Eyrefield Pride*
- Grey Duiker
- Vervet Monkey
- Impala
- Giraffe
- Zebra
- Wildebeest
- Tree Squirrel
- Elephant
- Wart Hog
- Bat

BIRDS
- Giant Kingfisher
- Burchells's Coucal
- Martial Eagle
- Yellow-billed Kite

ANIMAL OF THE CHAPTER;

■ Wildebeest *(Connochaetes taurinus)*

Unusually a solitary wildebeest

Also called the brindled gnu, the star of a famous song by Flanders and Swann, "I'm a gnu". More from my childhood, more re-enforcement of the exotic nature of Africa.

Approximately, one and a quarter million of this species undertake the migration from the Serengeti across Masai Mara. Wildebeest is an ungulate, an antelope. They eat grass, so have to keep on the move.

Avoiding predators could mean a life lasting twenty years. The greatest danger is at birth. After an eight or nine month pregnancy the calf can stand immediately and move within two hours. The flotilla principle applies, get back with the herd, safety in numbers. Nearly all predators fancy a newly born calf.

Adults are quite large, achieving over four feet at the shoulder and weighing thirty stone. This means a good meal for a pride of lions.

Wildebeest have horns measuring two feet in length but have little defence against the collective cunning of a pride determined to gain a kill.

Chapter Seven

SATURDAY AFTERNOON

Saturday –   **Afternoon**
Weather –   **Scrumptious**

I f some drives have less of a penetrating thrill, that merely interest and stimulate, then this was at the other end of the excitement scale.

Immediately outside of the camp (consider the implications) were the three lionesses from the Eyrefield Pride. They were lying in some scrub just off the road, doing very little, apart from a necessary stretch and yawn. We left them to it and pursued the game which we hoped the lions would chase later. Our plan was to return to see if somnambulance had lifted by the end of the drive.

When we did get back to them, much later in the day, the girls were on the move. In darkness, a single file moved along the road. As, in effect, the road is effectively a dirt track it has the two advantages of being easier on the paws and helps hunting; vision is unbroken and it is soundless movement, no grass to rustle or twigs to step on by mistake. There was a problem with the chosen route; it was straight towards the

99

camp. Andrew, the ranger, radioed in to get the gatekeeper to safety, shut in his sentry box. Rumour said he refused to come out for three days.

Ladies-in-waiting

Our first ever sighting of a leopard was in the Sabi Sands Reserve, whilst staying at Savanna Lodge. The ranger had expressed a desire to find a leopard for us and, therefore, we had driven around for quite a while. He had just given up, so we were off to see hippopotamus, when an adult female leopard strolled up the road towards us. Incredible and she walked alongside the car. Had I been daft enough an outstretched arm would have meant my hand being nine inches from her. We slowly pursued her but she knew where she was going and ignored us.

Imperturbable and, thankfully not hungry

Thankfully, the lions veered away from the man in the guard house but sadly off Mala Mala land. Our participation finished there. It is, to be honest, slightly unnerving when they stop walking or spraying to look you in the eye as if to say, "Don't annoy me too much or I will stop pretending I don't realise there are edibles in that car".

The lions are great but the real star of the evening was a leopard known as the Newington Male. For the same reason as the lions he was on the road. Of course, the downside is that he is easy for potential prey to see him - evolution takes longer for creatures to adopt a road camouflage. The leopard moved steadily forward until Andrew tried to second guess his route. At this point the cat turned off and went into the bush. We followed. Occasionally he washed a part of his body but generally he set out to mark his territory and we watched, rapt.

This leopard is like many males of the species. He is rippling muscle and power. At his peak around nine years of age and expanding his domain, he weighed more than most men and would kill a human being in seconds. He is the prop forward of the animal world.

Eventually, the leopard went where we could not follow but this had been fifteen minutes of us in awe and thrill. Nobody could or should ever get bored of watching a creature like this one.

Leopard cleaning

The third member of the Big Five we came across was a single, injured male buffalo. He was carrying his rear right leg. The reason was not immediately evident. Possibly it would heal or possibly he would become a target for lions. If he was a member of a herd he would soon drop off the pace, lose them and become highly vulnerable. Solitude makes them fair game and immobility accentuates the problems. For a man on foot a grumpy old male is bad news. No warning, just a smack and a gore.

The hippopotamus is not in the Big Five because they were never a favourite of big game hunters. Too easy to hit perhaps, too heavy to transport or too ugly to mount the head on a wall, but more dangerous than the other animals if you block one from either its young or the water in which it feels safe.

The specimen we found on this drive was in the scrub rather than in water and he was unhappy and very uncooperative. All pictures were obscured and we had to accept his indifference to our ambitions. It reminded us that this is not an orchestrated photo shoot or zoo.

In the bird stakes we were blessed by a sighting of the white-backed night heron. We had never seen one before and the ranger said it was rarely seen. It is a species vulnerable to extinction. The word night in its name may be a clue here.

Driving along the roads at night means many bugs are seen, as the headlights reflect off them. The very strong tip is keep your mouth closed. If you have to yawn do put your hand in front of your mouth. This is not only polite but saves a creepy-crawly from death by digestion and you from a horrid experience, a choking fit and three weeks worrying about infectious diseases.

Quizzical baboon - primate looking for a playmate

Dinner was served on the veranda and talk of the day's excitement and hopes for tomorrow. For a lucky few (not me) there was a late sighting of the genet cat which lived under the building. If you love nature the experience never stops.

Baboons were roosting fifteen yards from the diners. Parents scold their young as they try to settle for the night. For them this is a safe retreat from larger animals which might see them as a way of varying their diet. Leopards love a primate.

Trainee ranger Wayne had joined us for the first time. A lucky mascot? Certainly, a lucky man this day. Truly, an afternoon that would take some beating.

MAMMALS

- Impala
- Lions *Eyrefield Pride*
- Wildebeest
- Baboon
- Elephant
- Kudu
- Nyala
- Buffalo
- Scrub Hare
- Giraffe
- Leopard
- Hippopotamus

BIRDS

- Fork-tailed Drongo
- Pied Wagtail
- Spotted Dikkop
- Redbilled Woodhoopoe
- White-backed Night Heron

ANIMAL OF THE CHAPTER

■ Africa or Cape Buffalo (*Syncerus caffer*)

One buffalo has not quite got the hang of look out

The largest ungulate and a proper meal for a pride of lions. However, this is a creature which can look after itself and the herd will act together to repel predators which see calves as fair game. Bulls do become solitary and are more vulnerable to attack. Rarely could an animal appear more docile and yet have such a violent nature. It is rumoured a buffalo will, if injured, deliberately loop back to enact revenge. The weapons are the horns which can be over three feet long, combined with the buffalos size (six feet to the shoulder and eleven in length, weighing eight tons).

After a gestation of nearly a year one calf is born. As ever it is in high peril at this time.

A buffalo has poor eyesight and hearing but a highly attuned sense of smell. So presumably lions stink, which allows many of the species to live through to its natural lifespan of twenty plus.

It is a generalisation but size does matter in the wild.

Zebra mother and child could not be closer

Chapter Eight

SUNDAY MORNING

Sunday –   **Morning**
Weather –   **Exquisite**

So, yesterday afternoon's drive couldn't be bettered? It took eleven hours to disprove that hypothesis.

Ranger Andrew received a message over the radio - african or cape hunting dogs in the Mala Mala reserve. It is estimated there are only about three hundred and fifty of them in the whole of southern Africa. They are not territorial, so they move around constantly. And when they run, they keep going at pace. The message was they were lying down, resting. We needed to get there fast. From our position further in the north of the reserve it was quite a distance to cover. Nothing must stop us.

Of course, this single mindedness would be challenged if, for example, there was a leopard with a kill up a tree. Not going to happen? It did. We stopped to see the residue of an impala wedged in the high branches. The leopard, the Jakkalsdraan female, was lying contentedly nearby. We were an irrelevance in the life of a well fed cat. Eight years old, in her prime and looking great, we wanted to stay to observe her next move. Ordinarily, this could have been an hour well spent and potentially much longer. But had the wild dogs awoken? Were they on the move?

We had to go.

Nothing else could slow us unless we encountered a huge herd of elephants with numerous babies. So, we did. Any other time joy unconstrained.

Get out of the way you Neanderthal throwbacks.

Andrew knew a way around. Not on the map, it is called improvisation - the art of a ranger.

Simple question, "Are we in time?" A Land Rover came in the opposite direction. Dogs on the move.

So? And? "There's one". Yes, yes.

A pack of ten. And do they run! In five minutes they had left - blended, merged, evaporated. Gone. We saw them, photographed them, delighted in our luck. We had the bird in the hand, two in the bush and still had time to catch sight of a third in the scrub.

Wild dogs before they start running

If I had to say which, of all our experiences, was the most exciting the answer would have to be our two flights above the Masai Mara in a hot air balloon.

Being awoken even earlier than usual to ensure we were in the air at daybreak, first we needed to be transported to a nearby camp. Our residence was Governor's Camp and the flight was from Little Governors'. So, in pitch dark we rumbled along, still vainly looking for wildlife. To reach the second camp the River Mara has to crossed, still in the dark, on a boat resembling an ancient punt, from which the member of staff hangs on to a wire and pulls us over. Presumably the crocodiles were just waiting for the moment a mistake is made.

The balloons were laid out flat on a large clearing waiting to be inflated. As the burners were lit the nervous excitement grew. Gradually the shape of the balloon emerged. We boarded. The basket accommodated twelve irrespective of individual bulk. Our pilot was Ellie, a female driver. No jokes were made or appropriate.

At Ellie's command the holding ropes were released. Initially imperceptible, lift off happened very naturally. There was no vibration, only a sense of the land becoming more distant. There was noise, the burners are fierce. As the clearing wasn't very big Ellie had to gain height quickly, trees were looming. Her professionalism meant we were able to float just feet above the tops of the trees. Generally, we didn't go very high because that would limit the animal spotting opportunities. The height of the basket side was well above our centre of gravity, which gave a real sense of security. I do not have a great head for heights but this was no problem at all.

As Ellie killed the burner it was almost silent. We drifted. Clouds move less smoothly. Another burst of fire, a few feet gained. Our sister balloon dropped nearly to the ground and then burst upwards. The pilots were trying to give us the full treat.

To the east, as we were flying south, a glimmer of light quickly became a sun behind a hill and then it poked its head above the horizon; and then it was dawn, a new day. We were already well into our day. The rest of the world slept as we loved a life highlight. Few clouds interrupted, the sun showed a landscape erupting from a night, a time of violence and carnage in the wild. What would we see?

Being up here was a high quality adventure. Seeing sunrise made it special. Now if we could see some animals...

Two male lions were ignoring a car which appeared to be inches from them - maybe a facet of our height.

A family of hippos wallowing with crocodiles lying on the bank as we criss-crossed the Mara River.

Lines of galloping wildebeest and zebra. Perhaps I am dumb but I assumed the migration meant they all constantly moved in one direction. It is far more higgledy-piggledy and random. Why does one line sprint away, whilst another group chews the cud in an unconcerned manner? Who says move, who says, like Corporal Jones, "Don't panic"? Isn't panic the only way to survive? I suppose two million animals on the move cannot be orchestrated.

Giraffe and elephants could be seen ambling through the woods.

Numerous antelope grazed; reedbuck, waterbuck, impala.

Ballooning at sunrise

Topi took their comic position; two adults mount mounds of earth to keep watch, each one looking in the opposite direction over the other's shoulder. It works.

Warthogs scurried in the distance. They do not like balloons.

A family of hyenas ran along in the strange way that they seem to arc their bodies.

Ostriches disdainfully strode in isolation.

Vultures sat in trees, waiting to be vile.

The hour evaporated. Ellie gave us our instructions for landing. It boils down to ram your knees into the basket and hang on for your preservation. "It could be bumpy. There are termite hills", said the woman with our lives in her hands. She is an honest person.

Landing a balloon without brakes

On our first flight, the balloon scattered hundreds of wildebeest as we careered towards the land. Our speed appeared to increase. Relativity. We hit the ground and lifted off again. We hit again and bounced, and bounced and dragged. There are no brakes, just friction. We slowed and toppled over. The last few yards travelled horizontally.

Then stationary and nothing broken. Given the lack of local snakes, we were happy.

I extracted myself and was able to help my family out as well. The chasing cars arrived to take us to breakfast.

Disappointingly, the second time we flew we landed upright.

Breakfast was in the middle of nowhere. A table was set up. After a glass of something like champagne, there was coffee, bacon, sausages, cheese, bread…a final bonus was the black kites flying above us. The staff had positioned spears around the table to defend the food. Of course, as we finished, we were allowed to throw food into the air for the birds to swoop and catch. Unadulterated grace and velocity. Then a two hour game drive back to camp. Could it be bettered?

The River Sand has crocodiles. Today we saw one, or least its eyes. Then it slipped into the depths of the water. A good spot but not enough evidence to write an innovative thesis on animal behaviour.

The Hamerkop Corner resident crocodile

A dark chanting goshawk aware of everything

The best view of a bird on this drive was a dark chanting goshawk. It sat at the top of a foliage free tree, clearly visible and proud to be so. It looked at us, we looked at it and we moved on. He wasn't going to shift. Arrogance birdified.

A general observation would be that the number of butterflies demonstrates the purity of the atmosphere and the overall environment. There are many in Mala Mala. Vivid reds, greens and yellows, these insects are omnipresent. Perhaps not as spectacular as a big cat or graceful as a soaring raptor with its wings spread, but these little creatures quietly hugely enhance the experience.

Back on the patio at the camp, breakfast was accompanied by the grunting of hippos. In the distance one adult could be seen poking the top of its head out of the river. Then a whole animal emerged less than twenty yards from the camp boundary. We have seen hippos many times at various lodges at night but this was broad daylight. Another treat for us.

MAMMALS

- Impala
- Giraffe
- Elephant
- Leopard
- Kudu
- Rhinoceros
- Grey Duiker
- African Hunting Dog
- Zebra
- Tree Squirrel
- Baboon

REPTILES

- Bell's Hinged Tortoise
- Crocodile

BIRDS

- Green Wood-Hoopoe
- Black-headed Oriole
- Dark Chanting Goshawk

ANIMAL OF THE CHAPTER

- Cape Hunting Dogs or African Wild Dogs *(Lycaon pictus)*

Wild dog blending into the foliage

This is a species with different behaviour patterns. Wild Dogs are more successful hunters than the other mammalian predators; they kill at the end of eighty per cent of chases. Their prey is usually impala, gazelles and other medium sized antelopes. However, the dogs also take on zebra, wildebeest and other larger creatures. The plan is one dog holds the tip of the tail, another grabs the prey's upper lip and others disembowel whilst still alive. This is learned behaviour. It has been observed, however, this is a quicker process than throttling by lion or leopard.

After a kill, animals that have eaten may return to fellow pack members, such as pups or a mother looking after her litter, to regurgitate food for them.

The hierarchy is based on submission, instead of dominance. Dogs beg each other for food and to avoid aggression. Injury for a pack member would be a severe problem for an animal which runs for survival. The loss of one adult could cause issues for the balance of the pack, especially if there is a litter of pups to support.

Each pack has a male and female leader. If the father of the pack isn't with them it isn't necessarily the next eldest who takes over, it can be a young but mature animal. The female is likely to be the mother of the other females. If a death of either leader occurs the pack may split. There are examples of groups coming together but this is often temporary.

Natural life span is approximately ten years for this animal.

Chapter Nine

SUNDAY AFTERNOON

Sunday — **Afternoon**
Weather — **Wondrous**

ess than five minutes from the camp is a ford across the Sand River. Every day we saw two hamerkops patiently waiting for a fish dinner. Their nest, which was huge, was in a tree a hundred yards away. The nest was easily big enough for three up, three down plus en suite bathrooms. It was an amazing structure.

On this outing, as we arrived at Hamerkop Corner, there were also a crocodile, pied kingfisher, giant kingfisher, a sandpiper, blacksmith plover and three-banded plover. Lots of movement, except the crocodile, nervous energy being expended. This was a location to sit with binoculars, a flask of tea and some sandwiches. Previously at this place we had also seen green-backed heron, grey heron and numerous LBJ's flying past. LBJ was a bird watcher's code for unidentifiable small birds - Little Brown Jobs.

Very close to the edge of the camp we re-encountered the Styx lion pride. As ever the aged male was well to the rear. It appeared he only had four teeth left and, therefore, was a very

A lion that is reaching his final weeks

long way from prime condition. This pride had become more nomadic as they sought to avoid confrontation with ambitious younger males.

Sadly, the eldest lioness was injured. It looked like a broken front left leg. She was just able to place it on the ground when walking but running was a three legged exercise. On her own it would have meant death by starvation. However, as the rest of the pride was predominantly her daughters, they were accommodating her. The leg would improve and given the other lions could provide food in the meantime the old lady might recover. It is a harsh world these animals inhabit.

Again, we observed a group of wild creatures co-operating. The main body of the pride were always checking on the less able elders. They stopped, took a pause and then, when satisfied contact was maintained, move forward. The pride slowly moved northwards and we were unable to follow. It was definitely the last time we would see the old male but it was impossible not to hope the damaged lioness would survive. Human emotions but the pride also appeared very concerned. Maybe, there are deep connections between the cats.

We were "on a run". Luck was with us. Immediately, we found a leopard. It was one of the two sisters we had seen earlier in the week. She was on the prowl as dusk came in. Methodically, silently and deliberately she moved down the road. Easy to both thrill and admire, a killing machine but astonishingly beautiful. Leopards were always Alison's favourite. Less abundant than lions, more powerful than cheetahs, they live their lives in solitude generally. Independent and confident, leopards are impossible not to love.

We watched this glorious animal until she went off road and blended into her surroundings. Little wonder small antelopes, hares, birds and rodents fall foul of leopards. Actually, some of the antelopes are not small. Leopards are strong, climbing and carrying weights is not an issue. No other cat can climb like them.

The rangers are so good that whilst it would be a significant exaggeration to say we have seen everything, we have seen a lot. Yet, occasionally there is a real surprise. On a drive out of Savanna Paddy, the ranger, was delighted because a pair of honey badgers ran across the road and cavorted in the grass.

"These are very rare," he said. In fact, this was the only time we ever saw one. Looking like a cross between a badger (not a shock) and a skunk it is also known as a ratel. They are quite aggressive; as a smaller creature in the wild, if it had a passive persona, it would be extinct rapidly.

The steenbok is not a glamorous animal. We saw one on this drive and in doing so ensured we had seen more live ones than dead. They are slight, barely a snack for a big cat but cats are opportunistic.

Steenboks are diurnal, they feed and are active during the day. At night they survive by remaining stationary. To find the one we saw in its mouth, the lion would have had to have stumbled over it. A very unlucky steenbok but it is the way of nature. We can't turn carnivores into herbivores. Vegetarianism is not an option for lions, leopards and cheetahs.

The night had arrived. We returned towards camp via Hamerkop Corner again. On the bank above the river, Andrew stopped the car and turned off the lights. It was a moonless night. Whilst the darkness was not absolute it was very dark. There was a hint of the tree line but no more. It gave us a chance to gaze at the stars. Or more accurately the stars and the planet Venus. Previously, on safaris we have also seen Jupiter and, amazingly to me, a man made satellite travel across the sky.

That night there was a clear view of the Milky Way and it was stupendous. This is light which left its source thousands of years ago and only now do we see it. In this blackout it was possible to get a little of a sense of the vast, unimaginable number of stars there are in our galaxy. This was a real highlight of the whole adventure. It also emphasised that we cannot know there isn't life somewhere else. Maybe there was life and it has been extinguished. We are making a pretty good effort to spoil our own world. What a prize for the last person alive; all of the wealth will be his or hers. Please don't let certain megalomaniacs know or they will try to speed up the processes.

Andrew started the engine and turned on the headlights. The spell was broken but there was a surprise; stood next to the vehicle was a hyena. We hadn't heard it arrive. It reinforced the realisation I would not survive minutes on my own, on foot. This is the animal with the strongest jaws in the African bush and it could easily have grabbed a carelessly placed limb.

Coincidentally, the most graphic was left to last. At Hamerkop Corner three adult hippos were near the ford, in the river. There were also two babies, one of which was believed to be less than one week old. It explained the grunting going on through the day, which we heard whilst relaxing between drives. Mom was keeping little one in order. Hippos are not vulnerable to much but a baby is. Crocodiles and lions would be very interested. We were goo-gooing as if it was the cutest human baby we had ever seen.

One of the hippos got out of the water, saw the hyena which had followed us to the water, became spooked and threw itself back into the river. This was a belly flop in extremis. A tidal wave was created. There wasn't a crocodile to break his leap, so no damage was done.

It was time for a pre-dinner drink and further discussions of our fortune, our excitement and the disappointment that it would be home time tomorrow.

Dinner was in the Boma. Most camps prefer to use their Boma, an outdoor facility allowing visitors to continue the intense experience. A Boma is an enclosed, circular structure with a round of tables - a sophisticated barbeque. The quality of the food remains very good.

Twice we sat listening to approaching thunderstorms, the lightning vivid and threatening. The power of nature graphically displayed. It can be cold at certain times of the year but never cold enough to abandon a chilled beer or glass of wine or two.

MAMMALS
- Giraffe
- Grey Duiker
- Lions *Styx Pride*
- Tree Squirrel
- Rhinoceros
- Impala
- Steenbok
- Zebra

- Leopard
- Scrub Hare
- Hippopotamus
- Hyena

REPTILES
- Crocodile
- Chameleon

BIRDS
- African Hoopoe
- White-crowned Shrike
- Brown Headed Parrot
- Blackbellied Korhaan
- Common Sandpiper

ANIMAL OF THE CHAPTER
- Spotted Hyena *(Crotura crotura)*

Scavengers - hyena and vultures

There are four species of hyena, this is the biggest and most well known. This is the animal that seems to laugh.

It is perceived hyenas are scavengers but reality is they are very effective hunters too. However, a hyena will not walk past a meal if there is a chance of stealing it from another creature. To assist hunting hyenas possess good eyesight, hearing and sense of smell.

Males are typically about four feet long and two and a half feet to the shoulder. Less typical is the fact the female is larger than the male. She is also dominant. They live in small groups, but large numbers are not exceptional, and they act in a concerted manner.

Each clan has a hierarchy in which fully mature males are at the bottom, even below cubs and certainly subservient to females. Hyenas do not fight each other to the death or serious injury.

The female's reproductive system is unique. She has a pseudo-penis, an erect phallus. Because penetration needs complete compliance from the female it means only the male she wants will be allowed to mate.

Yellow Billed Hornbills

Chapter Ten

MONDAY MORNING

Monday –	**Morning**
Weather –	**Grey but mild**

W ell, the weather summed up our mood. Why does time pass so much more quickly when you are enjoying yourself than if you are bored? It seems daft but we would all recognise it as a truism. Our tenth and final drive of the holiday. I wrote then, "until the next time". That wasn't to happen for Alison but she could never have enjoyed a safari more than this one.

For the first time it was only Alison and myself as paying guests, with Andrew and Marka. It was to be a journey of ungulates and birds. I have already said birds enhance the experience. Loving big cats is great but I see them as special extras. There is a tremendous amount of beauty, colour and character beyond. On this trip we saw three of the larger birds.

The white-backed vulture is a vile individual. Aggressive and self-centred, it frequents the sites of death. One impala's loss, one leopard's leftovers equals one (or more) vultures being able to do that which they do best - picking at bones. Nothing is too trivial to reject. However, a vulture in flight is impressive. The wide wingspan and the slow rhythmical beat of the wings, as it moves from one lookout point to another, has panache.

The secretary bird looks and moves like a man in a bird costume. They always run away from us, thereby giving strong evidence that;

1   They cannot fly or

2   They don't want you to get too near and to be able to see the fraud

Secretary bird

Encouragingly, a major part of their diet is snakes.

Thirdly, we saw two groups of ground hornbills. These are big boys and girls. Black bodied, with red heads these birds prefer to walk rather than fly. This demonstrates their arrogance.

Group one of four individuals were strolling down a road until we arrived. Eventually, they did take to flight to perch on a nearby tree. Their style was okay if a little laboured and it didn't appear they could fly very far.

Ground hornbills take a stroll

The second group were already in a tree. They gave off a sense of menace, huddling together. Perhaps a threat only if you are a cricket or grasshopper. Rather than vultures, ground hornbill appear more like the evil birds with Liverpudlian accents in the Disney cartoon of Rudyard Kipling's Jungle Book.

We saw numerous antelopes and large herbivores but the excitement had been scaled in the preceding days. The strange elegance and poise of giraffes cannot be ignored. Physically astonishing a giraffe is like some people in that individual parts aren't pretty but the whole package is very attractive, laconic and relaxed.

Slightly regrettably, we returned to camp on a route which by-passed Hamerkop Corner. A last chance missed.

Literally, as we entered camp there was a small group of vervet monkeys chattering in the trees. They were taking the mickey out of those people who had to leave this paradise on earth. Primates are intelligent and a number of the camps we have visited have enjoyed the presence of cheeky monkeys.

127

Giraffes amble amongst the wildebeest

Vervet monkeys in the camp at Tanda Tula

They hang around in the trees waiting for an opportunity. It may be food, it may be things that glisten. "Do not feed the monkeys", is both an instruction and a plea from the heart issued by members of staff. Monkeys require no encouragement. Their knowledge has increased to a point at which these supposedly less intelligent creatures than us can even unzip tents if not fastened properly.

Monkeys bring the camp to life. For us these animals are a positive influence on life in the bush.

WHAT TO TAKE

- As little as possible, this is not a fashion parade.
- Layers of clothing which are not bright (greens and browns are best)
- Spectacles/contact lenses and spares - if you need them
- Sunglasses
- Binoculars
- Camera/batteries/film/re-charger
- Video camera plus accessories
- Broad brimmed hat
- Sunblock
- Torch
- Alarm
- Medical kit
- Book of animals
- Reading matter

Try to leave the laptop and phone at home or at least switched off. It is amazing my mobile phone has worked in the middle of the bush.

MAMMALS

- Kudu
- Bushbuck
- Waterbuck
- Hippopotamus
- Elephant
- Giraffe
- Impala
- Dwarf Mongoose
- Grey Duiker
- Wildebeest
- Vervet Monkey (in the camp)

REPTILE

- Bell's Hinged Tortoise

BIRDS

- White-backed Vulture
- Grey Hornbill
- Secretary Bird
- Ground Hornbill

ANIMAL OF THE CHAPTER

- Giraffe *(Giraffa camelopardalis)*

A naturally funny giraffe

Everybody loves the giraffe. It is non-threatening and absolutely distinctive in appearance. This is the tallest land animal, the male often grows to eighteen feet. It is the neck which distinguishes the giraffe from all other creatures. Yet it only has the same seven vertebrae many animals have, just elongated.

The name giraffe translates as "fast walking". The length of legs can make it appear this doesn't seem to be the case. At full pace a giraffe can run at thirty five miles per hour. When running the front and rear legs move together, whereas in a walk the left and right legs are synchronised. The picture is made more incongruous by a head bobbing movement due to the front legs being ten percent longer than those at the back.

Giraffes sleep for only two hours each day. Half of their lives are dedicated to eating. Using their eighteen inch tongue giraffes browse from the branches of trees. The male (bull) tend to the higher levels and females (cow) take lower ones. Bulls will form bachelor herds and cows will congregate, typically

131

in groups of a dozen. Giraffes are prepared to mingle with other ruminants. So, at a waterhole or river a giraffe will drink alongside wildebeest and zebra, for example.

The only threat to adults, apart from man, is the lion. It is, however, unlikely a pride will try to take a fully grown giraffe if there are alternative food sources available. A kick from a giraffe can crush a lion's skull or break its back.

A calf is a different proposition for lions, hyenas and wild dogs. At times only a half of young giraffes make maturity. They are very vulnerable. After a gestation of fifteen months the newly born calf is born from a standing mother, which means the embryo sack falls six or seven feet to the ground. It can stand and suckle almost immediately and within a few hours can run.

If a giraffe can avoid hunters it can live to twenty five years of age.

Plenty of food for all as giraffe and zebra ignore us

It isn't easy to hide a giraffe

Elephants at the lodge

Chapter Eleven

JUST TRAVELLING

We visited southern Africa a number of times and whilst animals were the focus on each occasion we did travel more widely as well - mainly as a precursor to safari.

There is no point in going to Cape Town and then ignoring some of the best known sites in the world.

Table Mountain dominates the city. The advice is as soon as there is a clear day get up it immediately. We took a taxi to the cableway, which is two thirds of the way up the side of the mountain. A queue is inevitable but it is very efficiently dealt with and in no time we were swinging gently on our way up.

At the top there are panoramic views of the city, the ocean (including Robben Island) and the surrounding areas. No wildlife in sight, however.

To reach Robben Island means a boat trip. "Everyone" sees dolphins - we didn't but not because we weren't looking intently. This is the island on which Nelson Mandela and so many enemies of the apartheid state were incarcerated. To visit the prison is to glimpse the levels of inhumanity humanity can inflict upon itself. Our guide was a former inmate.

The cells are barren and during winter would have been stark. The tales are even more disgraceful, of barbarism and sadism. Prisoners made to run bear foot on tiles covered in water and soap, whilst whipped by guards. Broken bones were likely, medical treatment scant. Yet Nelson Mandela and others emerged with their dignity and principles intact. Nobody escaped as the swim to the mainland would be certain suicide - currents and sharks.

We did see a tortoise and springbok. I assume they had been shipped in by man.

The harbour in Cape Town has a number of cape fur seals which live a life of cosseted splendour. They are not underfed.

Penguins at Boulders Beach

Along the coast, Boulders Beach in Simonstown is the home to many jackass penguins, also known as african penguins. The title jackass is attributed due to the almost braying noise they make. The colony seems unperturbed by people, although one did peck my shoe furiously. I retreated; a close encounter with nature. These birds clearly feel at ease in this area as they create nests, lay eggs and return every year. Most people know the answer to the question, "Do polar bears eat penguins?" For the few who don't let me reveal they do not, mainly because they live thousands of miles from each other. The furthest north any penguin resides is in the Galapagos Islands, which are south of the Equator. Polar bears live in the northern hemisphere, towards or beyond the Arctic Circle.

A geographical and historical point is the Cape of Good Hope, the southernmost tip of the African continent. This is the location at which the South Atlantic Ocean meets the Indian Ocean. It is the vast collision of colossal forces of these great seas which makes rounding the Horn such a difficult proposition for ships. Naturally, there is a café as near as possible to the edge of the world. There is also a sign for all enthusiastic photographers and those with sceptical families.

This area is the Cape Point Nature reserve and does have some wildlife. We saw eland, hartebeest, baboons and ostriches. Tales tell that the baboons throw rocks at cars for amusement, the little monkeys.

One of the most delightful places we have ever stayed is Cybele Forest Lodge. The rooms, food and facilities are fabulous. It is situated in Mpumalanga, near the Kruger National Park and Sabi Sands. Mpumalanga means "Place of the Rising Sun". It is a plateau on the Drakensberg Escarpment as the highveld begins its fall to the lowveld.

The suites had all we could need. The grounds occupy three hundred acres of lush forest around which people can walk freely. Vicky Cushing and I took an hour long stroll

137

to see the Secret Pool, a weir and a waterfall. It is wild, so there are snakes and duiker but we saw none. Rumour said a leopard had been seen in the general area.

This was a very restful place and time for us. Alison loved it.

We first saw Knysna from the train as we crossed the Kaaismans Bridge. Three major points of interest inherent in this sentence;

- The train was powered by a steam engine. Trainspotters paradise, and that includes me. We had boarded at George, passed another similar train at Sedgefield and now approached the end of the line at Knysna. This is the Outeniqua Railway (The Outeniqua Choo Tjoe). At the terminus there is a roundtable. Anyone can stand within feet of the engine, smell the smoke, watch the engine turned, photograph from a thousand angles, smile at other people who don't give a damn that it is a "steamer". The bridge over the line gave me the chance to stand in the smoke as the engine passed below and allow my clothes to become permeated and gross. Awesome.

- Kaaismans Bridge is purportedly the most photographed bridge in the world. It is on thousands of calendars. The train comes down a hill, which is covered in lush vegetation, announcing its presence by smoke and wheel strain, disappears briefly, then emerges to cross the river and bend into the town.

■ Knysna is a cute town on the estuary of the Knysna River which flows out to the Indian Ocean through "The Heads". It is at the foot of the Outeniqua Mountains. This is a town based on fishing traditionally and tourism. There are many activities available including and especially eating and drinking.

We took a boat across the bay to the Featherbed Nature Reserve. It is a slightly testing walk around the reserve but beautiful and worthwhile. We saw little wildlife except a fish eagle.

A less inspiring place is Oudtshoorn, the ostrich capital of the world. You can see ostriches, ostrich feathers, ostrich eggs, models of ostriches, things made of ostrich feathers...you get the picture. And yet the marketing people try to make it sound attractive. There are ostrich museums, people who talk about ostriches, ostrich farms, ostrich conferences...

Alison actually rides an ostrich

The highlight is an ostrich farm. They avoid taking you to the abattoir. There is an inevitable well stocked curio shop; a chance to stand on an ostrich egg; an ostrich race; two old birds which are more or less tame to stand near; and genuinely entertaining a small person can ride an ostrich. Alison was small and keen. Whether the ostrich enjoyed the moment will never be known but Alison did. One of her famous animal encounters.

Ironically, an ostrich in the wild is a wonderful sight. Maybe as a member of a pair or merely alone, rarely has a bird looked less worried. Why? There are loads of potential problems. Perhaps lions think ostriches are boring.

Nearby are the Kango Caves, in the Swartberg Mountains. These are staggering with stalactites and stalagmites which have taken many thousands of years to form. These towering formations sit in vast halls. The caves are easily accessible and worth a trip, not two as I have enjoyed. Mary Minett and Nat referred to them as "The Devil's Caves" - I have no idea why. The guide said he wouldn't go any deeper as he hated the spiders.

From Londolozi we took two flights to Zambia via Johannesburg. The arrangements went very smoothly and we arrived fresh and keen to see The Falls. Would our American friends accept Victoria Falls as equal to Niagara? Everything is bigger and better in the good old U S of A, according to the patriotic yanks. In fairness, Jeff and Vicky are not stereotypical of Americans portrayed on TV. They are very well travelled, urbane and amusing. We first met on a cruise around South America and they, together with Terry and Susan Parry, made a great holiday even better. We also won a number of quizzes on that cruise, to the chagrin of fellow travellers. An exceedingly sad postscript is Jeff passed away in March 2009.

We landed at Livingstone. First we had to go to the hotel. The Stanley Safari Lodge is unique. Our room only had three walls, so we could lie in bed and look at the spray from the falls billow; there was nothing in front of us, no wall, window, nothing. We were open to the vagaries of the elements and passing animals. Our room had its own plunge pool. It was opulent, and we had it. This is literally and metaphorically a very long way from Midland Road, Cotteridge in Birmingham where I was born. I would never have thought, imagined or conceived I would be there. I couldn't actually have imagined such a place existed. For a little boy from a terraced house, even with a passion for fauna, to get anywhere as exotic as central Africa is not a reasonable expectation. I do not underestimate my good fortune and it was Alison who led me on these adventures. My ambitions would probably been satisfied by a week on an Italian beach (which I haven't done). How very, very lucky I am.

Zambesi at sunset

141

Having explored the room and the gardens which include a swimming pool from which the spray is still visible, we took a taxi to actually see the Victoria Falls. These are the most famous places discovered by Dr David Livingstone, the first European to see them. He found the falls in 1855. Henry Stanley was sent to look for Livingstone on behalf of the New York Herald, not an English newspaper and famously found him in the country now called Tanzania, on the shore of Lake Tangyanika. Apparently, the famous line, "Doctor Livingstone, I presume?" may be a figment of Stanley's hindsight. The relevant pages of his diary disappeared. A possible re-write of history, confident Livingstone would never return to civilisation to deny it.

The Zambesi cascades dramatically

The Victoria Falls are beyond description. Everyone should go if they have half-a-chance. Timing is everything as during the dry season the Zambezi is reduced to a trickle. We saw billions of gallons throwing themselves off the edge to cascade hundreds of feet to create a vast constant fury of spray and current.

The falls are magnificent in full flow. Even the spray level at the apex, where the river meets the drop, travels for hundreds of feet. At the entry gate we hired polythene cagoules. A wise selection, or not. Wrapped in our protection we descended the few steps for a complete view. We stood in true awe. This was a sight to inspire the most cynical heart. As we wound round the narrow path to see the deluge from different angles the falling water became heavier; and heavier; and heavier. It is mesmeric; a colossal force and majestic sight. The cagoules were totally irrelevant. We dripped, every inch of clothing saturated, our entire bodies drenched and we loved it. Alison's hair was always a source of great worry to her; it had to be perfect, yet she didn't care at all. This was one of those occasions when people laugh for no apparent reason, merely the joy of the experience. We strolled and looked, it was as simple as that. For how long we watched the tons of water topple to the lower river I don't know, time had stopped. A final joy was the second best rainbow we had ever seen. A full arch, so close the colours were completely defined. Another example of the natural being unbeatable. Just off the coast of the Hawaiian island of Kauai a total rainbow had bent into the sea within twenty yards of us magnificently. Presumably, if I had been a professional diver a pot of gold could have been acquired easily.

Eventually, we returned to the gate, left our "protective clothing" and headed for the inevitable market of local crafts, salesmen and charlatans. Buy items if you want them having bartered vigorously but do accept you have still been ripped off. Whilst there is real poverty in Zambia it isn't with these guys. If you want to make a contribution find another mechanism. We dried out naturally in no time, so the taxi wasn't damaged on the return trip to the hotel.

Needing the loo in the middle of the night was a nervy experience. Twenty yards padding bare footed to the facility and anything could have entered through the non-existent wall.

How brave I felt when the safety of bed was regained.

Jeff and Vicky crossed the bridge to Zimbabwe. Alison and I chose not to go, so as not to show any sympathy or support for the Mugabe regime. This disappointment was sharp because I have known a number of great people from Zimbabwe and it is reputed to be a beautiful country. It would have been another pin on the map of the world. The report back was of decay and poverty, even at this most fabulous tourist location.

The Zambezi River, another name to excite; another exotic name from the atlas; another unrealistic dream. Our trip was on a small cruiser with twenty other people. At this point the river is a couple of hundred yards wide. Small islands pop up in the middle of the waterway. The boat gently moved along one bank as we went up river and down the other towards the falls. Now, the captain has done this many, many times but what happens if the engine fails… I can imagine problems easily. There were no issues, just numerous birds. As with all tours there was a refreshment break, even though beers had already been passed

Hippos in the Zambesi

around the boat. We didn't land at a jetty but at a clearing on the bank. Literally, six feet from the boat was an inert crocodile. Not huge, about four feet long, a woman next to me laughed convinced it was a rubber blow-up facsimile. Her face changed as it slid in the river. Again, I ask the question, "Who is responsible for Health and Safety?" The crew knew animal behaviour well enough to recognise we were the threat, not the croc.

Back on the boat it was time to venture nearer to the falls. Showing off, the skipper opened the clutch and we flew. As we rounded a bend a hippopotamus thrust itself out of the water, mouth fully extended as a sign of aggressive warning. The boat swerved to avoid it and slowed to an appropriate speed. Had there been a large family of hippos it could have been different. As nothing untoward occurred we all chuckled. Swimming is not a great option in the Zambezi.

ANIMAL OF THE CHAPTER

■ Hippopotamus *(Hippopotamus amphibus)*

Hippos in Kenya

It is well known hippopotami kill more people in Africa than any other animal, despite being a herbivore. This is an aggressive creature.

Hippos live most of the day in the water, rivers or pools, with their eyes and nostrils just above the surface. Hardly an iceberg because ninety eight percent of two tons of animal are unseen. At night hippos graze on grass - lots of it. Surprisingly, hippos will travel five miles from their home base and safety in search of food. Hippos are ugly. Unfortunate but true, large bloated body on short, squat legs yet they can run at thirty miles per hour. A man is in trouble if he upsets one. One bite by the two feet long teeth is death.

As ever, man is a problem. Hippos are culled for ivory and meat. Only lions are a threat to adult hippos in the wild. A pride can bring one down but it isn't a frequent occurrence.

On a number of occasions we have walked near to grazing hippos. There has been no recognition of our presence. Hippos are short sighted.

The research tells us hippos live in groups between five and thirty. In Kenya there was a group of well over fifty during the day, in the river; a remarkable sight.

Inevitably, hippo young are subject to the interests of some carnivores. Crocodiles, lions and hyenas are especially an issue. As crocodiles share the same stretch of water, the violent nature of a hippo is understandable.

With the hippopotamus everything, except eating, happens in the water. Conception for the female is under water, with brief breathing concessions. After eight months baby arrives in the water and suckling is often below the surface. Should a hippo survive to adulthood it may well live to forty years old.

EPILOGUE

Alison Ball (nee Moss) died on 16th February 2008, one month after her 50th birthday and four months after our 25th Wedding Anniversary. She was conscious for both events but they couldn't be joyous occasions. However, I am convinced that knowing they were approaching did help Alison focus and reach them.

There were three good things during Alison's eight months of illness;

1 I saw a great deal more of my daughter than I would have done ordinarily.

2 People were fantastic. We could not have asked for more support and understanding.

3 I was able to stop buying the Daily Mail. Alison was a very caring person but with slightly strange political views, so insisted on it as her choice of one of our newspapers. I will not be buying that particular organ again.

Throughout Alison's medical problem we tried to be very positive. Even when she was unconscious in Queen Elizabeth Hospital, Birmingham we talked, played games and laughed. The television was on or the CD playing.

We went through a life changing event, so I have changed my life. To perpetuate her memory Natalie, Alison's brother Gregor and I have created a company to pursue our joint interests such as animal conservation, environmental issues, travel, theatre and supporting deserving people. We have called our business, Naturally Concerned (for Alison) Limited.

This is our vehicle for continuing the positive approach to Alison's life. The website is (not surprisingly) www.naturallyconcerned.com

We are delighted there is a leopard at the AfriCat Foundation in Namibia called Alison and a cheetah in the wild named Mrs B following sponsorship we have taken out from the kind contributions in the collection at the funeral service, and Nigel and Mary Minett's generosity.

This is a description of our times in Africa. It hasn't allowed me to reflect on orang utans in Borneo and Alison's paper tissue being grabbed by a baby known as Tiger Woods, whales in the South Pacific and the Azores, paddling with dolphins in Hawaii and riding an elephant in Sri Lanka. I did receive an offer of a million camels as a payment for Alison whilst we were in Egypt. Clearly, I wasn't allowed to accept it, although it would have been interesting to see the million produced.

If our lives are to have meaning we must have principles and purpose. We have described ours. We also intend to have fun. Clearly, life is too short to waste time on irrelevant worries. There are many key issues to address but there is no law which states we can't enjoy ourselves at the same time.

It is time to consider the broader implications of our actions, time to stimulate the soul.

Alison loved Africa, wild animals, our cats, her friends, her family and Natalie especially. Maybe Naturally Concerned (for Alison) will be an effective medium to make a small impact on our world and allow people to remember Alison through her passions.

To quote St. Augustine, "The World is a book, and those who do not travel read only one page."

We are naturally concerned.

As we turned a corner there was an elephant waiting

TOO LATE?

The cat ran through the bush

Speed and grace but no sound

As if God had ordained a hush

And in it the cat gave a silent bound.

On its own, at little threat

As a breed perhaps some years.

Mankind owes a debt

Just years, then the tardy tears.

Extinct, a final roar

Cheetah - once vulnerable, now no more.